WILLIAM SHAKESPEARE

# The Tragedy of
# Antony and Cleopatra

EDITED BY MAYNARD MACK

PENGUIN BOOKS

BALTIMORE · MARYLAND

This edition first published 1960
Reprinted 1961, 1962
Penguin Books Inc.
3300 Clipper Mill Road, Baltimore 11, Maryland

*Copyright © 1960
by Penguin Books Inc.*

*Library of Congress Catalog Card
Number 59-9123*

*Printed in the United States of America*

# CONTENTS

# SHAKESPEARE AND HIS STAGE

William Shakespeare was christened in Holy Trinity Church, Stratford-on-Avon, April 26, 1564. His birth is traditionally assigned to April 23rd. He was the eldest of four boys and two girls who survived infancy in the family of John Shakespeare, glover and trader of Henley Street, and his wife Mary Arden, daughter of a small landowner of Wilmcote. In 1568 John was elected Bailiff (equivalent to Mayor) of Stratford, having already filled the minor municipal offices. The town maintained for the sons of the burgesses a free school, taught by a university graduate and offering preparation in Latin sufficient for university entrance; its early registers are lost, but there can be little doubt that Shakespeare received the formal part of his education in this school.

On November 27, 1582, a license was issued for the marriage of William Shakespeare (aged eighteen) and Ann Hathaway (aged twenty-six), and on May 26, 1583, their child Susanna was christened in Holy Trinity Church. The inference that the marriage was forced upon the youth is natural but not inevitable; betrothal was legally binding at the time, and was sometimes regarded as conferring conjugal rights. Two additional children of the marriage, the twins Hamnet and Judith, were christened on February 2, 1585. Meanwhile the prosperity of the elder Shakespeares had declined, and William was impelled to seek a career outside Stratford.

The tradition that he spent some time as a country teacher is old but unverifiable. Because of the absence of records his early twenties are called the "lost years," and only one thing about them is certain — that at least some of these years were spent in winning a place in the acting profession. He may have begun as a provincial trouper, but by 1592 he was established in London and prominent enough to be attacked. In a pamphlet of that year, *Groatsworth of Wit*, the ailing Robert Greene complained of the neglect which university writers like himself had suffered from actors, one of whom was daring to set up as a playwright:

> ... an upstart crow beautified with our feathers, that with his *Tiger's heart wrapt in a player's hide* supposes he is as well able to bombast out a blank verse as the best of you, and being an absolute Johannes-factotum, is in his own conceit the only Shake-scene in a country.

The pun on his name, and the parody of his line "O tiger's heart wrapt in a woman's hide" (*III Henry VI*), pointed clearly to Shakespeare. Some of his admirers protested, and Henry Chettle, the editor of Greene's pamphlet, saw fit to apologize:

> I am as sorry as if the original fault had been my fault, because myself have seen his demeanor no less civil than he excellent in the quality he professes. Besides divers of worship have reported his uprightness of dealing, which argues his honesty, and his facetious grace in writing that approves his art. (Prefatory epistle, *Kind Heart's Dream*)

The plague closed the London theatres for many months in 1593–94, denying the actors their livelihood. To this period belong Shakespeare's two narrative poems, *Venus and Adonis* and *Rape of Lucrece*, both dedicated to the Earl

8

of Southampton. No doubt the poet was rewarded with a gift of money as usual in such cases, but he did no further dedicating and we have no reliable information on whether Southampton, or anyone else, became his regular patron. His sonnets, first mentioned in 1598 and published without his consent in 1609, are intimate without being explicitly autobiographical. They seem to commemorate the poet's friendship with an idealized youth, rivalry with a more favored poet, and love affair with a dark mistress; and his bitterness when the mistress betrays him in conjunction with the friend; but it is difficult to decide precisely what the "story" is, impossible to decide whether it is fictional or true. The real distinction of the sonnets, at least of those not purely conventional, rests in the universality of the thoughts and moods they express, and in their poignancy and beauty.

In 1594 was formed the theatrical company known until 1603 as the Lord Chamberlain's Men, thereafter as the King's Men. Its original membership included, besides Shakespeare, the beloved clown Will Kempe and the famous actor Richard Burbage. The company acted in various London theatres and even toured the provinces, but it is chiefly associated in our minds with the Globe Theatre built on the south bank of the Thames in 1599. Shakespeare was an actor and joint owner of this company (and its Globe) through the remainder of his creative years. His plays, written at the average rate of two a year, together with Burbage's acting won it its place of leadership among the London companies.

Individual plays began to appear in print, in editions both honest and piratical, and the publishers became increasingly aware of the value of Shakespeare's name on the title pages. As early as 1598 he was hailed as the leading English dramatist in the *Palladis Tamia* of Francis Meres:

As Plautus and Seneca are accounted the best for Comedy and Tragedy among the Latins, so Shakespeare among the English is the most excellent in both kinds for the stage: for Comedy, witness his *Gentlemen of Verona*, his *Errors*, his *Love labors lost*, his *Love labors won* [*Taming of the Shrew?*], his *Midsummers night dream*, & his *Merchant of Venice;* for Tragedy, his *Richard the 2, Richard the 3, Henry the 4, King John, Titus Andronicus*, and his *Romeo and Juliet.*

The note is valuable, both in indicating Shakespeare's prestige and in helping us to establish a chronology. In the second half of his writing career, history plays gave place to the great tragedies; and farces and light comedies gave place to the problem plays and symbolic romances. In 1623, seven years after his death, his former fellow actors, John Hemming and Henry Condell, cooperated with a group of London printers in bringing out his plays in collected form. The volume is generally known as the First Folio.

Shakespeare had never severed his relations with Stratford. His wife and children may sometimes have shared his London lodgings, but their home was Stratford. His son Hamnet was buried there in 1596, and his daughters Susanna and Judith were married there in 1607 and 1616 respectively. (His father, for whom he had secured a coat of arms and thus the privilege of writing himself gentleman, died in 1601, his mother in 1608.) His considerable earnings in London, as actor-sharer, part owner of the Globe, and playwright, were invested chiefly in Stratford property. In 1597 he purchased for £60 New Place, one of the two most imposing residences in the town. A number of other business transactions, as well as minor episodes in his career, have left documentary records. By 1611 he was in a position to retire, and he seems gradually to have withdrawn from theatrical activity in order to live in Stratford. In March, 1616, he made a will, leaving token bequests to Burbage, Hemming, and Condell, but the bulk of his estate to his family. The most famous feature of the will, the bequest of the second-best bed to his wife, reveals nothing about Shakespeare's marriage; the quaintness of the provision seems commonplace to those familiar with ancient testaments. Shakespeare died April 23, 1616, and was buried in the Stratford church where he had been christened. Within seven years a monument was erected to his memory on the north wall of the chancel. Its portrait bust and the Droeshout engraving on the title page of the First Folio provide the only likenesses with an established claim to authenticity. The best verbal vignette was written by his rival Ben Jonson, the more impressive for being imbedded in a context mainly critical:

> ... I loved the man, and do honor his memory (on this side idolatry) as much as any. He was indeed honest, and of an open and free nature: he had an excellent fancy, brave notions, and gentle expressions. . . . (*Timber or Discoveries*, c. 1623–30)

The reader of Shakespeare's plays is aided by a general knowledge of the way in which they were staged. The King's Men acquired a roofed and artificially lighted theatre only toward the close of Shakespeare's career, and then only for winter use. Nearly all his plays were designed for performance in such structures as the Globe—a three-tiered amphitheatre with a large rectangular platform extending to the center of its yard. The plays were staged by daylight, by large casts brilliantly costumed, but with only a minimum of properties, without scenery, and quite possibly without intermissions. There was a rear stage balcony for action "above," and a curtained rear recess for "discoveries" and other special effects, but by far the major portion of any play was enacted upon the projecting platform, with episode following episode in swift succession, and with shifts of time and place signaled the audience only by the momentary clearing of the stage between the episodes. Information about the identity of the characters and, when necessary, about the time and place of the action was incorporated in the dialogue. No additional indications of place have been inserted in the present editions; these are apt to obscure the original fluidity of structure, with the emphasis upon action and speech rather than scenic background. The acting, including that of the youthful apprentices to the profession who performed the parts of women, was highly skillful, with a premium placed upon grace of gesture and beauty of diction. The audiences, a cross section of the general public, commonly numbered a thousand, sometimes more than two thousand. Judged by the type of plays they applauded, these audiences were not only large but also perceptive.

## THE TEXTS OF THE PLAYS

About half of Shakespeare's plays appeared in print for the first time in the folio volume of 1623. The others had been published individually, usually in quarto volumes, during his lifetime or in the six years following his death. The copy used by the printers of the quartos varied greatly in merit, sometimes representing Shakespeare's true text, sometimes only a debased version of that text. The copy used by the printers of the folio also varied in merit, but was chosen with care. Since it consisted of the best available manuscripts, or the more acceptable quartos (although frequently in editions other than the first), or of quartos corrected by reference to manuscripts, we have good or reasonably good texts of most of the thirty-seven plays.

In the present series, the plays have been newly edited from quarto or folio texts depending, when a choice offered, upon which is now regarded by bibliographical specialists as the more authoritative. The ideal has been to reproduce the chosen texts with as few alterations as possible, beyond occasional relineation, expansion of abbreviations, and modernization of punctuation and spelling. Emendation is held to a minimum, and such material as has been added, in the way of stage directions and lines supplied by an alternative text, has been enclosed in square brackets.

None of the plays printed in Shakespeare's lifetime were divided into acts and scenes, and the inference is that the author's own manuscripts were not so divided. In the folio collection, some of the plays remained undivided, some were divided into acts, and some were divided into acts and scenes. During the eighteenth century all of the plays were divided into acts and scenes, and in the Cambridge edition of the mid-nineteenth century, from which the influential Globe text derived, this division was more or less regularized and the lines were numbered. Many useful works of reference employ the act-scene-line apparatus established by the Globe text.

Since the act-scene division thus established is obviously convenient, but is of very dubious authority so far as Shakespeare's own structural principles are concerned, or the original manner of staging his plays, a problem is presented to modern editors. In the present series the act-scene division of the Globe text is retained marginally, and may be viewed as a reference aid like the line numbering. A printer's ornament marks the points of division when these points have been determined by a cleared stage indicating a shift of time and place in the action of the play, or when no harm results from the editorial assumption that there is such a shift. However, at those points where the established division is clearly misleading – that is, where continuous action has been split up into separate "scenes" – the ornament is omitted and the distortion corrected. This mechanical expedient seemed the best means of combining utility and accuracy.

*The General Editor.*

# INTRODUCTION

Critics have been known to speak of *Macbeth, King Lear,* and *Antony and Cleopatra* as Shakespeare's *Inferno, Purgatorio,* and *Paradiso.* The comparison is misleading if taken as a guide to Shakespeare's states of mind, of which we know nothing, or even as a guide to the order of the three plays, the consensus of modern opinion being that *Macbeth* (c. 1606) falls between *King Lear* (c. 1605) and *Antony and Cleopatra* (c. 1607). But the notion has a certain merit if taken solely as a guide to tone.

*Macbeth* and *King Lear,* like *Othello* earlier, are dark plays, filled with actions taking place in what can only be called "dramatic" as well as literal night, a dark night of the soul engulfed by evil. *Antony and Cleopatra,* on the other hand, is a bright play. *Macbeth* and *King Lear,* too, are savage – if one fully responds to them, terrifying. There is no savagery in *Antony and Cleopatra;* it is moving, exhilarating, even exalting, but contains nothing that should tear an audience to tatters. The humor of *Macbeth* and *King Lear* is either grim or pitiful: a drunken porter at the gate of hell, a court jester shivering on a stormy heath. The humor of *Antony and Cleopatra* is neither grim nor pitiful, although sometimes acrid enough. Cleopatra is given qualities that make her a very unqueenly queen: she lies, wheedles, sulks, screams, and makes love, all with equal abandon. Antony is given qualities that make him in some senses more like an elderly playboy than a tragic hero. We are encouraged by Shakespeare in this play to disengage ourselves from the protagonists, to feel superior to them, even to laugh at them, as we rarely are with his earlier tragic persons.

Against laughter, however, the playwright poises sympathy and even admiration. Tawdry though he has made these seasoned old campaigners in love and war, he has also magnified and idealized them, to the point at which their mutual passion becomes glorious as well as cheap. Antony, the play tells us, has "infinite virtue," Cleopatra "infinite variety." He is the "triple pillar of the world," she is the "day o' th' world." He seems a "plated Mars," she more beautiful than Venus. His guardian spirit is called "unmatchable," she is called a "lass unparalleled." He descends from the god Hercules, she from the moon-goddess Isis. She sees him as the sun and moon, lighting this "little O, th' earth"; Charmian sees her as the "Eastern star." When Antony cries Ho! "Like boys unto a muss, kings would start forth"; Cleopatra has a hand that "kings Have lipped, and trembled kissing." When Antony will swear an oath, he cries, "Let Rome in Tiber melt and the wide arch Of the ranged empire fall!" When Cleopatra will swear, she cries, "Melt Egypt into Nile! and kindly creatures Turn all to serpents." Antony, about to die, thinks of death as a continuing amour with Cleopatra: "Where souls do couch on flowers, we'll hand in hand, And with our sprightly port make the ghosts gaze." When Cleopatra is about to die, she sees death in the same transcendent terms: "Go, fetch My best attires. I am again for Cydnus, To meet Mark Antony."

Traces of Shakespeare's duality of attitude toward his lovers may be found in Plutarch, whose *Lives of the Noble Grecians and Romans Compared Together* he had read in Thomas North's magnificent English rendering (1579) of Jacques Amyot's translation of the original into French (1559). So eloquent was North's prose that in certain instances it could be assumed into blank verse with a minimum of change, as in the following well-known description of Cleopatra going to meet Antony in her barge, which should be compared with the lines of Enobarbus (II, ii, 191–241) in Shakespeare's play.

. . . She went to Antonius at the age when a woman's beauty is at the prime, and she also of best judgment. . . . She disdained to set forward otherwise but to take her barge in the river of Cydnus, the poop whereof was of gold, the sails of purple, and the oars of silver, which kept stroke in rowing after the sound of the music of flutes, hautboys, cithers, viols, and such other instruments as they played upon in the barge. And now for the person of herself: She was laid under a pavilion of cloth-of-gold of tissue, apparelled and attired like the goddess Venus commonly drawn in picture; and hard by her, on either hand of her, pretty fair boys, apparelled as painters do set forth god Cupid, with little fans in their hands, with the which they fanned wind upon her. Her ladies and gentlewomen also, the fairest of them, were apparelled like the nymphs Nereides (which are the mermaids of the waters) and like the Graces, some steering the helm, others tending the tackle and ropes of the barge, out of the which there came a wonderful passing sweet savor of perfumes that perfumed the wharf's side, pestered with innumerable multitudes of people. Some of them followed the barge all alongest the river's side, others also ran out of the city to see her coming in, so that in the end there ran such multitudes of people one after another to see her that Antonius was left post-alone in the market place in his imperial seat to give audience. And there went a rumor in the people's mouths that the goddess Venus was come to play with the god Bacchus for the general good of all Asia.

Shakespeare's play owes to Plutarch's life of Antony many of its incidents, and to North's prose the wording of occasional passages like the lines of Enobarbus referred to above. It precipitates, however, an interpretation of these materials that is spectacularly Shakespeare's own. Plutarch's narrative, for all its stress on the baffling blends of vice and virtue in great minds, is at bottom the relatively familiar story of the Great Man and the Temptress. His Antony loses the world for love, not wisely but too well, and his Cleopatra, though possibly she rises to genuine love before the end (Plutarch leaves this point undecided), is rather the instrument of a great man's downfall than a tragic figure in herself. To understand the distinctiveness of Shakespeare's treatment of her, we have only to return to the passage in Plutarch and the lines of Enobarbus already cited. Plutarch's Cleopatra is all siren, every effect calculated to ensnare the senses of the conquering Roman. Shakespeare's Cleopatra is all siren too, but she is more. The repeated paradoxes in Enobarbus's language serve notice on us that everything about her is impossible, mysteriously contradictory. Her page-boys cool her cheeks only to make them burn, "and what they undid did." Her gentlewomen are seeming mermaids, half human, half sea-creature. The silken tackle swells with a life of its own at "the touches of those flower-soft hands." The wharves come alive and have "sense," quickened by her "strange invisible perfume." The city comes alive, to "cast" its people out upon her. Antony is left sitting in the market place, whistling to the air, and the air itself, except that nature abhors a vacuum, would have "gone to gaze on Cleopatra too" and left a gap behind. She is a creature, says Enobarbus in conclusion, who makes defect perfection, and, when breathless, power breathes forth. Other women cloy the appetites they feed, "but she makes hungry Where most she satisfies." Even the vilest things are so becoming when she does them that "the holy priests Bless her when she is riggish."

This is clearly not a portrait of a mere intriguing woman, but a kind of absolute oxymoron: Cleopatra is glimpsed here as a force like the Lucretian Venus, whose vitality resists both definition and regulation. Yet enveloped as she is by Enobarbus's mocking tones, wise and faintly world-weary, calculating amusedly the effects of his words on these uninitiated Romans, she remains the more a trollop for that. His reliable anti-romanticism undercuts the picture he draws of her, and at the same time confirms it, because it comes from him.

The ambiguity of these lines extends to almost every-thing in the play. In the world the dramatist has given his lovers, nothing is stable, fixed, or sure, not even ultimate values; all is in motion. Seen from one point of view, the motion may be discerned as process, the inexorable march of causes and effects, exemplified in Antony's fall and epitomized by Caesar in commenting to Octavia on the futility of her efforts to preserve the peace: "But let de-termined things to destiny Hold unbewailed their way." Seen from another angle, the motion reveals itself as flux, the restless waxing and waning of tides, of moons, of human feeling. Especially of human feeling. Antony pur-sued Brutus to his death, we are reminded by Enobarbus, yet wept when he found him slain. So within the play itself Caesar weeps, having pursued Antony to his death; and Antony, desiring that Fulvia die, finds her "good, being gone"; and Enobarbus, seeking some way to leave his master, is heart-struck when he succeeds; and the Roman populace, always fickle, "Like to a vagabond flag upon the stream, Goes to and back, lackeying the varying tide, To rot itself with motion."

In such a context, it is not surprising that the lovers' passion is subject to vicissitudes, going to and back in ever more violent oscillations of attraction and recoil. Shakespeare nowhere disguises the unstable and ultimately destructive character of their relationship, and those who, like Shaw, have belabored him for not giving sexual infatuation the satiric treatment it deserves have read too carelessly. It is likewise not surprising that the play's structure should reflect, in its abrupt and numerous shifts of scene, so marked a quality of its leading characters – their emotional and psychological vacillation. Though these shifts have also met with criticism, some finding in them a serious threat to unity, they are easily seen in the theatre to be among the dramatist's means of conveying to us an awareness of the competing values by which the lovers, and particularly Antony, are torn. "Kingdoms are clay," he declares in Egypt; "The nobleness of life Is to do thus," and embraces Cleopatra. A few hours later, however, he says with equal earnestness, "These strong Egyptian fetters I must break Or lose myself in dotage," and he departs for Rome. Again, he declares to Octavia in Rome, hereafter everything shall "be done by th' rule," yet scarcely thirty lines later, after his interview with the soothsayer, he has added, "I will to Egypt." From this point on follows a succession of fluctuations in both war and love. In war, confidence of victory shifting to despair at loss, then to new confidence, then to new despair. In love, adorings of Cleopatra changing to recriminations, then to renewed adorings, then to fresh disgust. This aspect of the play's rhythm is vividly summed up in two speeches in the third act (III, xi). "I have offended reputation," Antony says after the first sea defeat, "A most unnoble swerving": there is the voice of Rome and the soldier. A few seconds after, he says to Cleopatra, "Fall not a tear, I say: one of them rates All that is won and lost": this is the voice of Egypt and the lover.

"All that is won *and* lost" is of course the crucial ambiguity of this tragedy. Perhaps it is one about which no two readers are likely finally to agree. Much is obviously lost by the lovers in the course of the play, and Shakespeare underscores this fact, as Plutarch had done, by placing their deaths in Cleopatra's monument – that is to say, a tomb. All those imperial ambitions that once mustered "the kings o' th' earth for war" have shrunk now to this narrow stronghold, which is also a waiting grave. Antony had said as he put his arms about Cleopatra in the opening scene, "Here is my space." Now that challenge has been taken up. This is his space indeed.

But what then, if anything, has been won? The answer to this question depends as much on what one brings to *Antony and Cleopatra* as on what one finds there, for the evidence is mixed. Antony does give his life for his love before the play ends, and we observe that there are no recriminations at his final meeting with Cleopatra; only his quiet hope that she will remember him for what was noblest in him, and her acknowledgment that he was, and is, her man of men. But then, too, his death has been precipitated by her duplicity in the false report of hers; it has among its motives a self-interested desire to evade Caesar's triumph; and the suicide is even bungled in the doing: if this is a hero's death, it is a humiliating one. Likewise, Cleopatra seems to give her life for love. As Antony will be a bridegroom in his death, "and run into't As to a lover's bed," so Cleopatra will be a bride in hers, calling, "Husband, I come," receiving darkness as if it were "a lover's pinch, Which hurts, and is desired," and breathing out, in words that could equally be describing the union of life with death or the union of lover with lover, "As sweet as balm, as soft as air, as gentle – O Antony!" This, however, is the same woman who has long studied "easy ways to die," who ends her life only after becoming convinced that Caesar means to lead her in triumph, and who has cached away with her treasurer Seleucus more than half her valuables in case of need. True, the scene with Seleucus can be so played as to indicate that she is using his confession to dupe Caesar about her intention to die. But that is precisely the point. What the actor or reader makes of her conduct here will be conditioned by what he has made of her elsewhere, by what he makes of the play as a whole, and even, perhaps, by his beliefs about human nature and the depiction of human nature in art.

Are we to take the high-sounding phrases which introduce us to this remarkable love affair in the play's first scene as amorous rant?

*Cleopatra*. If it be love indeed, tell me how much.
*Antony*. There's beggary in the love that can be reckoned.
*Cleopatra*. I'll set a bourn how far to be beloved.
*Antony*. Then must thou needs find out new heaven, new earth.

Or is there a prophetic resonance in that reference to "new heaven, new earth," which we are meant to remember when Cleopatra, dreaming of a transcendent Antony –

His face was as the heav'ns, and therein stuck
A sun and moon, which kept their course and lighted
The little O, th' earth. . . .
His legs bestrid the ocean: his reared arm
Crested the world: his voice was propertied
As all the tunèd spheres –

22

consigns her baser elements to "baser life"? Does the passion of these two remain a destructive element to the bitter end, doomed like all the feeling in the play "to rot itself with motion"? Or, as the world slips from them, have they a glimmering of something they could not have earlier understood, of another power besides death "Which shackles accidents and bolts up change"? Is it "paltry to be Caesar," as Cleopatra claims, since "Not being Fortune, he's but Fortune's knave"? Or is it more paltry to be Antony, and, as Caesar sees it, "give a kingdom for a mirth," as well as, eventually, the world?

To such questions, *Antony and Cleopatra,* like life itself, gives no clear-cut answers. Shakespeare holds the balance even, and does not decide for us who finally is the strumpet of the play, Antony's Cleopatra, or Caesar's Fortune, and who, therefore, is the "strumpet's fool." Those who would have it otherwise, who are "hot for certainties in this our life," as Meredith phrased it, should turn to other authors than Shakespeare, and should have been born into some other world than this.

*Yale University*                                    MAYNARD MACK

Note on the text: *Antony and Cleopatra* was first published in the folio of 1623, in a good text with full stage directions, evidently printed from Shakespeare's own draft after it had been prepared for stage production. The present edition closely follows the folio text, admitting only the most generally accepted emendations: I, ii, 4 *charge* (F *change*), I, ii, 106 *minds* (F *winds*), I, iv, 44 *deared* (F *feared*), I, iv, 46 *lackeying* (F *lacking*), I, v, 61 *man* (F *man's*), II, i, 41 *warred* (F *wan'd*), II, vii, 110 *bear* (F *beat*), III, xiii, 74 *deputation* (F *disputation*). The folio text is undivided into acts and scenes. The division appearing marginally in the present edition is that of the Globe text; it is supplied for the purpose explained above in the general introduction.

## [Names of the Actors

Mark Antony ⎫
Octavius Caesar ⎬ triumvirs
M. Aemilius Lepidus ⎭

Sextus Pompeius

Domitius Enobarbus ⎫
Ventidius ⎪
Eros ⎪
Scarus ⎬ friends to Antony
Decretas ⎪
Demetrius ⎪
Philo ⎭

Canidius, lieutenant-general to Antony

Maecenas ⎫
Agrippa ⎪
Dolabella ⎪
Proculeius ⎬ friends to Caesar
Thidias ⎪
Gallus ⎭

Taurus, lieutenant-general to Caesar

Menas ⎫
Menecrates ⎬ friends to Pompey
Varrius ⎭

Roman Officer under Ventidius

A Schoolmaster, ambassador from Antony to Caesar

Alexas ⎫
Mardian ⎪
Seleucus ⎬ attendants on Cleopatra
Diomedes ⎭

A Soothsayer

A Clown

Cleopatra, Queen of Egypt

Octavia, sister to Caesar and wife to Antony

Charmian ⎫
Iras ⎬ attendants on Cleopatra

Officers, Soldiers, Messengers, Attendants]

# THE TRAGEDY OF
# ANTONY AND CLEOPATRA

❧

*Enter Demetrius and Philo.*

*Philo.* Nay, but this dotage of our general's
  O'erflows the measure: those his goodly eyes
  That o'er the files and musters of the war
  Have glowed like plated Mars, now bend, now turn
  The office and devotion of their view             5
  Upon a tawny front. His captain's heart,
  Which in the scuffles of great fights hath burst
  The buckles on his breast, reneges all temper
  And is become the bellows and the fan
  To cool a gypsy's lust.

  *Flourish. Enter Antony, Cleopatra, her Ladies, the Train,*
    *with Eunuchs fanning her.*

                    Look where they come:    10
Take but good note, and you shall see in him
The triple pillar of the world transformed
Into a strumpet's fool. Behold and see.

I, i, 1 *dotage* (applicable not only to the aged; Antony 'dotes' on Cleopatra)
4 *plated* armored  5 *office* service  6 *front* face (with pun on military
sense)  8 *reneges* rejects  *temper* moderation  10 *gypsy* (1) native o Egypt
(gypsies were thought to originate thence) (2) slut  12 *The triple . . . world*
one of the three 'pillars' of the world (the others being Octavius Caesar
and Lepidus)  13 *fool* dupe

*Cleopatra.* If it be love indeed, tell me how much.
15 *Antony.* There's beggary in the love that can be reckoned.
*Cleopatra.* I'll set a bourn how far to be beloved.
*Antony.* Then must thou needs find out new heaven, new
    earth.

*Enter a Messenger.*

*Messenger.* News, my good lord, from Rome.
*Antony.*                              Grates me! The sum.
*Cleopatra.* Nay, hear them, Antony.
20 Fulvia perchance is angry; or who knows
    If the scarce-bearded Caesar have not sent
    His pow'rful mandate to you, 'Do this, or this;
    Take in that kingdom, and enfranchise that.
    Perform't, or else we damn thee.'
*Antony.*                              How, my love?
25 *Cleopatra.* Perchance? Nay, and most like:
    You must not stay here longer, your dismission
    Is come from Caesar; therefore hear it, Antony.
    Where's Fulvia's process? Caesar's I would say? both?
    Call in the messengers. As I am Egypt's Queen,
30 Thou blushest, Antony, and that blood of thine
    Is Caesar's homager: else so thy cheek pays shame
    When shrill-tongued Fulvia scolds. The messengers!
*Antony.* Let Rome in Tiber melt and the wide arch
    Of the ranged empire fall! Here is my space,
35 Kingdoms are clay: our dungy earth alike
    Feeds beast as man. The nobleness of life

16 *bourn* limit  18 *Grates...sum* it annoys me; be brief  20 *Fulvia* Antony's
wife  21 *scarce-bearded* hardly grown up (Octavius was 23)  23 *Take in*
seize  *enfranchise* set free  26 *dismission* recall  28 *process* summons  31 *Is
Caesar's homager* pays respect to Caesar's authority  *else* or else  34 *ranged*
well-ordered (?) wide-ranging (?)

Is to do thus; when such a mutual pair
And such a twain can do't, in which I bind,
On pain of punishment, the world to weet
We stand up peerless.
*Cleopatra.*                    Excellent falsehood!          40
Why did he marry Fulvia, and not love her?
I'll seem the fool I am not. Antony
Will be himself.
*Antony.*                    But stirred by Cleopatra.
Now for the love of Love and her soft hours,
Let's not confound the time with conference harsh.          45
There's not a minute of our lives should stretch
Without some pleasure now. What sport to-night?
*Cleopatra.* Hear the ambassadors.
*Antony.*                         Fie, wrangling queen!
Whom every thing becomes — to chide, to laugh,
To weep; whose every passion fully strives          50
To make itself, in thee, fair and admired.
No messenger but thine, and all alone
To-night we'll wander through the streets and note
The qualities of people. Come, my queen;
Last night you did desire it. — Speak not to us.          55
               *Exeunt [Antony and Cleopatra] with the Train.*
*Demetrius.* Is Caesar with Antonius prized so slight?
*Philo.* Sir, sometimes when he is not Antony
He comes too short of that great property
Which still should go with Antony.
*Demetrius.*                         I am full sorry
That he approves the common liar, who          60

37 *thus* (perhaps indicating an embrace; perhaps a general reference to
their way of life)  39 *weet* know  42 *the fool . . . not* i.e. foolish enough to
believe you  45 *confound* destroy, waste  46 *stretch* pass  50 *passion* mood
56 *prized* valued  58 *property* distinction  60 *approves* confirms

27

Thus speaks of him at Rome; but I will hope
Of better deeds to-morrow. Rest you happy!       *Exeunt.*

I, ii     *Enter Enobarbus, Lamprius, a Soothsayer, Rannius, Lu-*
          *cillius, Charmian, Iras, Mardian the Eunuch, and*
          *Alexas.*

    *Charmian.* Lord Alexas, sweet Alexas, most anything
Alexas, almost most absolute Alexas, where's the soothsayer that you praised so to th' Queen? O that I knew
this husband which, you say, must charge his horns
5   with garlands!

    *Alexas.* Soothsayer!

    *Soothsayer.* Your will?

    *Charmian.* Is this the man? Is't you, sir, that know things?

    *Soothsayer.* In nature's infinite book of secrecy
    A little I can read.

10  *Alexas.*                   Show him your hand.

    *Enobarbus.* Bring in the banquet quickly: wine enough
    Cleopatra's health to drink.

    *Charmian.* Good sir, give me good fortune.

    *Soothsayer.* I make not, but foresee.

15  *Charmian.* Pray then, foresee me one.

    *Soothsayer.* You shall be yet far fairer than you are.

    *Charmian.* He means in flesh.

I, ii, S.D. *Enter Enobarbus . . . Alexas* (thus in folio, but Lamprius, Rannius,
and Lucillius do not speak in the scene and do not appear elsewhere in the
play. Possibly Lamprius is the name of the Soothsayer.)  2 *absolute* perfect
4–5 *must . . . garlands* i.e. must be not only a cuckold and grow horns (as
cuckolds—husbands of unfaithful wives—were humorously said to do) but
a champion cuckold, wearing a winner's garland  17 *He . . . flesh* he means
that you will put on weight

28

*dramatizes the atmosphere.
morally free society.*

*Iras.* No, you shall paint when you are old.

*Charmian.* Wrinkles forbid!

*Alexas.* Vex not his prescience, be attentive.                    20

*Charmian.* Hush!

*Soothsayer.* You shall be more beloving than beloved.

*Charmian.* I had rather heat my liver with drinking.

*Alexas.* Nay, hear him.

*Charmian.* Good now, some excellent fortune. Let me be 25
married to three kings in a forenoon and widow them
all. Let me have a child at fifty, to whom Herod of Jewry
may do homage. Find me to marry me with Octavius
Caesar, and companion me with my mistress.

*Soothsayer.* You shall outlive the lady whom you serve.    30

*Charmian.* O excellent! I love long life better than figs.

*Soothsayer.* You have seen and proved a fairer former
    fortune
Than that which is to approach.

*Charmian.* Then belike my children shall have no names.
Prithee, how many boys and wenches must I have?    35

*Soothsayer.* If every of your wishes had a womb,
And fertile every wish, a million.

*Charmian.* Out, fool! I forgive thee for a witch.

*Alexas.* You think none but your sheets are privy to your
wishes.                    40

*Charmian.* Nay, come, tell Iras hers.

*Alexas.* We'll know all our fortunes.

*Enobarbus.* Mine, and most of our fortunes, to-night, shall
be — drunk to bed.

23 *heat . . . drinking* i.e. rather than with unreciprocated love (the liver
being regarded as love's residence)   27–28 *to . . . homage* i.e. to whom even
King Herod (who massacred the infants of Judea) would do homage
29 *companion me with* give me as my servant   32 *proved* experienced
34 *have no names* be illegitimate   35 *wenches* girls   38 *I . . . witch* i.e. I can
see that you have no prophetic powers   39 *privy to* in on the secret of

29

45  *Iras.* There's a palm presages chastity, if nothing else.
    *Charmian.* E'en as the o'erflowing Nilus presageth famine.
    *Iras.* Go, you wild bedfellow, you cannot soothsay.
    *Charmian.* Nay, if an oily palm be not a fruitful prognos-
    tication, I cannot scratch mine ear. Prithee tell her but
50  a workyday fortune.
    *Soothsayer.* Your fortunes are alike.
    *Iras.* But how, but how? Give me particulars.
    *Soothsayer.* I have said.
    *Iras.* Am I not an inch of fortune better than she?
55  *Charmian.* Well, if you were but an inch of fortune better
    than I, where would you choose it?
    *Iras.* Not in my husband's nose.
    *Charmian.* Our worser thoughts Heavens mend! Alexas —
    come, his fortune, his fortune. O, let him marry a
60  woman that cannot go, sweet Isis, I beseech thee, and
    let her die too, and give him a worse, and let worse
    follow worse till the worst of all follow him laughing
    to his grave, fiftyfold a cuckold. Good Isis, hear me this
    prayer, though thou deny me a matter of more weight:
65  good Isis, I beseech thee.
    *Iras.* Amen, dear goddess, hear that prayer of the people.
    For, as it is a heartbreaking to see a handsome man loose-
    wived, so it is a deadly sorrow to behold a foul knave
    uncuckolded. Therefore, dear Isis, keep decorum, and
70  fortune him accordingly
    *Charmian,* Amen.
    *Alexas.* Lo now, if it lay in their hands to make me a

---

48 *oily palm* (symptom of sensuality)   48–49 *fruitful prognostication* prophetic sign of fertility   50 *workyday* ordinary   60 *go* bear children (?) give
—or receive—sexual satisfaction (?)   *Isis* Egyptian goddess of earth, fertility, and the moon   67–68 *loose-wived* married to a loose woman   69 *keep
decorum* i.e. act as befits a goddess

aspect of Egypt — exalted                    30

cuckold, they would make themselves whores but they'ld
do't.

*Enter Cleopatra.*

*Enobarbus.* Hush, here comes Antony.
*Charmian.*                                   Not he, the Queen. 75
*Cleopatra.* Saw you my lord?
*Enobarbus.*                       No, lady.
*Cleopatra.*                                   Was he not here?
*Charmian.* No, madam.
*Cleopatra.* He was disposed to mirth; but on the sudden
   A Roman thought hath struck him. Enobarbus!
*Enobarbus.* Madam?                                             80
*Cleopatra.* Seek him, and bring him hither. Where's Alexas?
*Alexas.* Here at your service. My lord approaches.

*Enter Antony with a Messenger [and Attendants].*

*Cleopatra.* We will not look upon him. Go with us.
         *Exeunt [all but Antony, Messenger, and Attendants].*
*Messenger.* Fulvia thy wife first came into the field.
*Antony.* Against my brother Lucius?                          85
*Messenger.* Ay.
   But soon that war had end, and the time's state
   Made friends of them, jointing their force 'gainst Caesar,
   Whose better issue in the war from Italy
   Upon the first encounter drave them.
*Antony.*                                   Well, what worst? 90
*Messenger.* The nature of bad news infects the teller.

74 S.D. (this, the folio's, placing of Cleopatra's entrance suggests either that
the sound of her approach is heard before she can be seen, thus causing Enobarbus's error, or that his remark is ironical, alluding to her power over
Antony's will)  87 *time's state* conditions of the moment  89 *issue* success
90 *drave* drove

*Antony.* When it concerns the fool or coward. On.
Things that are past are done with me. 'Tis thus:
Who tells me true, though in his tale lie death,
I hear him as he flattered.

95 *Messenger.*                    Labienus
(This is stiff news) hath with his Parthian force
Extended Asia: from Euphrates,
His conquering banner shook, from Syria
To Lydia and to Ionia,
Whilst —

*Antony.*     Antony, thou wouldst say.

100 *Messenger.*                              O, my lord.

*Antony.* Speak to me home, mince not the general tongue,
Name Cleopatra as she is called in Rome:
Rail thou in Fulvia's phrase, and taunt my faults
With such full license as both truth and malice
105 Have power to utter. O, then we bring forth weeds
When our quick minds lie still, and our ills told us
Is as our earing. Fare thee well awhile.

*Messenger.* At your noble pleasure.     *Exit Messenger.*

*Antony.* From Sicyon, how the news? Speak there!

110 *1. Attendant.* The man from Sicyon — is there such an one?

*2. Attendant.* He stays upon your will.

*Antony.*                              Let him appear.
These strong Egyptian fetters I must break
Or lose myself in dotage.

---

95 *as* as if  *Labienus* Quintus Labienus, who had been sent by Brutus and
Cassius to seek aid against Antony and Octavius Caesar from Orodes, King
of Parthia, and was now commanding a Parthian army  97 *Extended* seized
101 *home* plainly  *mince . . . tongue* don't soften what everybody is saying
104 *license* freedom  106 *quick* live, fertile  107 *earing* being ploughed
(to uproot the weeds)  110, 111 *1. Attendant, 2. Attendant* (folio reads
'1. Messenger, 2. Messenger')  111 *stays upon* awaits

*Enter another Messenger, with a letter.*

What are you?

Messenger. Fulvia thy wife is dead.

Antony.                         Where died she?

Messenger. In Sicyon.                                        115
    Her length of sickness, with what else more serious
    Importeth thee to know, this bears.        *[Gives a letter.]*

Antony.                    Forbear me.    *[Exit Messenger.]*
    There's a great spirit gone! Thus did I desire it:
    What our contempts doth often hurl from us,
    We wish it ours again. The present pleasure,                120
    By revolution low'ring, does become
    The opposite of itself: she's good, being gone;
    The hand could pluck her back that shoved her on.
    I must from this enchanting queen break off:
    Ten thousand harms, more than the ills I know,            125
    My idleness doth hatch.

*Enter Enobarbus.*

How now, Enobarbus!

Enobarbus. What's your pleasure, sir?

Antony. I must with haste from hence.

Enobarbus. Why, then we kill all our women. We see how   130
    mortal an unkindness is to them. If they suffer our
    departure, death 's the word.

Antony. I must be gone.

Enobarbus. Under a compelling occasion let women die.

---

113 s.d. (apparently anticipated in folio by 'Enter another Messenger'
after l. 108)   117 *Importeth* concerns   118 *Forbear* leave   121 *By revolution
low'ring* i.e. moving downward on the revolving wheel of our opinions
124 *enchanting* (Cleopatra is felt by the Romans in the play to have witch-
like powers of seduction)   126 *idleness* trifling

135   It were pity to cast them away for nothing, though
      between them and a great cause they should be esteemed
      nothing. Cleopatra, catching but the least noise of this,
      dies instantly: I have seen her die twenty times upon far
      poorer moment. I do think there is mettle in death,
140   which commits some loving act upon her, she hath such
      a celerity in dying.

*Antony.* She is cunning past man's thought.

*Enobarbus.* Alack, sir, no; her passions are made of nothing
      but the finest part of pure love. We cannot call her
145   winds and waters sighs and tears: they are greater storms
      and tempests than almanacs can report. This cannot be
      cunning in her; if it be, she makes a shower of rain as
      well as Jove.

*Antony.* Would I had never seen her!

150   *Enobarbus.* O, sir, you had then left unseen a wonderful
      piece of work, which not to have been blest withal
      would have discredited your travel.

*Antony.* Fulvia is dead.

*Enobarbus.* Sir?

155   *Antony.* Fulvia is dead.

*Enobarbus.* Fulvia?

*Antony.* Dead.

*Enobarbus.* Why, sir, give the gods a thankful sacrifice.
      When it pleaseth their deities to take the wife of a man
160   from him, it shows to man the tailors of the earth;
      comforting therein, that when old robes are worn out,
      there are members to make new. If there were no more
      women but Fulvia, then had you indeed a cut, and the
      case to be lamented. This grief is crowned with consolation,

---

139 *moment* cause   *mettle* vigor   147 *makes* manufactures   148 *Jove* i.e.
Jupiter Pluvius, Roman god of rain   160 *the tailors* i.e. that the gods are
the tailors   163–64, 169 (in *cut, case, business,* and *broached,* Enobarbus
puns bawdily)

34

your old smock brings forth a new petticoat, and indeed 165
the tears live in an onion that should water this sorrow.

*Antony.* The business she hath broachèd in the state
Cannot endure my absence.

*Enobarbus.* And the business you have broached here cannot
be without you; especially that of Cleopatra's, which 170
wholly depends on your abode.

*Antony.* No more light answers. Let our officers
Have notice what we purpose. I shall break
The cause of our expedience to the Queen
And get her leave to part. For not alone                          175
The death of Fulvia, with more urgent touches,
Do strongly speak to us, but the letters too
Of many our contriving friends in Rome
Petition us at home. Sextus Pompeius
Hath given the dare to Caesar and commands                        180
The empire of the sea. Our slippery people,
Whose love is never linked to the deserver
Till his deserts are past, begin to throw
Pompey the Great and all his dignities
Upon his son; who, high in name and power,                        185
Higher than both in blood and life, stands up
For the main soldier; whose quality, going on,
The sides o' th' world may danger. Much is breeding,
Which, like the courser's hair, hath yet but life
And not a serpent's poison. Say, our pleasure,                    190

---

167 *broachèd* opened up  171 *abode* staying  173 *break* tell  174 *expedience*
haste  176 *touches* motives  178 *contriving* i.e. acting in my interest  179 *at
home* to return home  *Sextus Pompeius* son of Pompey the Great, who had
been outlawed, but, owing to the division between Antony and Octavius
Caesar, was able to seize Sicily and command the Roman sea-routes
183 *throw* transfer  186 *blood and life* vital energy  187 *quality* character and
position  *going on* evolving  188 *danger* endanger  189 *courser's hair* (horse
hairs in water were thought to come to life as small serpents)

To such whose place is under us, requires
Our quick remove from hence.
*Enobarbus.*  I shall do't.                                      *[Exeunt.]*

I, iii              *Enter Cleopatra, Charmian, Alexas, and Iras.*

*Cleopatra.*  Where is he?
*Charmian.*                    I did not see him since.
*Cleopatra.*  See where he is, who's with him, what he does:
    I did not send you. If you find him sad,
    Say I am dancing; if in mirth, report
5   That I am sudden sick. Quick, and return. *[Exit Alexas.]*
*Charmian.*  Madam, methinks, if you did love him dearly,
    You do not hold the method to enforce
    The like from him.
*Cleopatra.*                    What should I do, I do not?
*Charmian.*  In each thing give him way, cross him in nothing.
10  *Cleopatra.*  Thou teachest like a fool: the way to lose him!
*Charmian.*  Tempt him not so too far. I wish, forbear.
    In time we hate that which we often fear.

                        *Enter Antony.*

But here comes Antony.
*Cleopatra.*                    I am sick and sullen.
*Antony.*  I am sorry to give breathing to my purpose —
15  *Cleopatra.*  Help me away, dear Charmian! I shall fall.
    It cannot be thus long; the sides of nature
    Will not sustain it.

---

191 *place* rank   I, iii, 3 *sad* serious   8 *I do not* that I am not doing   11
*Tempt* try   *I wish* I wish you would   14 *breathing* utterance   16 *sides of
nature* human body

*Antony.*                    Now, my dearest queen —
*Cleopatra.* Pray you stand farther from me.
*Antony.*                                   What's the matter?
*Cleopatra.* I know by that same eye there's some good news.
   What, says the married woman you may go?            20
   Would she had never given you leave to come!
   Let her not say 'tis I that keep you here.
   I have no power upon you: hers you are.
*Antony.* The gods best know —
*Cleopatra.*                          O, never was there queen
   So mightily betrayed: yet at the first            25
   I saw the treasons planted.
*Antony.*                       Cleopatra —
*Cleopatra.* Why should I think you can be mine, and true,
   (Though you in swearing shake the thronèd gods)
   Who have been false to Fulvia? Riotous madness,
   To be entangled with those mouth-made vows            30
   Which break themselves in swearing.
*Antony.*                                  Most sweet queen —
*Cleopatra.* Nay, pray you seek no color for your going,
   But bid farewell, and go: when you sued staying,
   Then was the time for words: no going then,
   Eternity was in our lips and eyes,            35
   Bliss in our brows' bent: none our parts so poor
   But was a race of heaven. They are so still,
   Or thou, the greatest soldier of the world,
   Art turned the greatest liar.
*Antony.*                       How now, lady?
*Cleopatra.* I would I had thy inches; thou shouldst know            40
   There were a heart in Egypt.

20 *the married woman* i.e. Fulvia    32 *color* pretext    33 *sued* begged for    36
*bent* curve    37 *race of heaven* of heavenly origin (?) of heavenly flavor (?)
41 *Egypt* Cleopatra

*Antony.*                 Hear me, Queen:
The strong necessity of time commands
Our services awhile, but my full heart
Remains in use with you. Our Italy
45   Shines o'er with civil swords; Sextus Pompeius
Makes his approaches to the port of Rome;
Equality of two domestic powers
Breed scrupulous faction; the hated, grown to strength,
Are newly grown to love; the condemned Pompey,
50   Rich in his father's honor, creeps apace
Into the hearts of such as have not thrived
Upon the present state, whose numbers threaten;
And quietness, grown sick of rest, would purge
By any desperate change. My more particular,
55   And that which most with you should safe my going,
Is Fulvia's death.

*Cleopatra.* Though age from folly could not give me
     freedom,
It does from childishness. Can Fulvia die?

*Antony.* She's dead, my queen.
60   Look here, and at thy sovereign leisure read
The garboils she awaked. At the last, best,
See when and where she died.

*Cleopatra.*             O most false love!
Where be the sacred vials thou shouldst fill
With sorrowful water? Now I see, I see,
65   In Fulvia's death, how mine received shall be.

*Antony.* Quarrel no more, but be prepared to know

44 *in . . . you* for you to keep and use   45 *civil swords* i.e. civil war   48 *scrupulous faction* contest over trifles   52 *state* government   53–54 *grown . . . change* i.e. ill through peace, would cure itself by letting blood   54 *particular* personal concern   55 *safe* make safe   61 *garboils* commotions   *best* best news of all   63–64 *sacred vials . . . water* (a reference to the practice of consecrating bottles of tears to the dead)

*Cleo is compared to the sun.*

The purposes I bear: which are, or cease,
As you shall give th' advice. By the <u>fire</u>
That quickens Nilus' slime, I go from hence     *image*
Thy soldier, servant, making peace or war  *of mud give*
As thou affects.     *both to life*     70

*Cleopatra.*          Cut my lace, Charmian, come;
But let it be, I am quickly ill, and well —
So Antony loves.

*Antony.*          My precious queen, forbear,
And give true evidence to his love, which stands
An honorable trial.

*Cleopatra.*          So Fulvia told me.     75
I prithee turn aside and weep for her;
Then bid adieu to me, and say the tears
Belong to Egypt. Good now, play one scene
Of excellent dissembling, and let it look
Like perfect honor.

*Antony.*          You'll heat my blood: no more.     80

*Cleopatra.* You can do better yet; but this is meetly.

*Antony.* Now by my sword —

*Cleopatra.*          And target. Still he mends.
But this is not the best. Look, prithee, Charmian,
How this Herculean Roman does become
The carriage of his chafe.     85

*Antony.* I'll leave you, lady.

*Cleopatra.*          Courteous lord, one word.
Sir, you and I must part, but that's not it:

---

68 *fire* i.e. the sun  69 *quickens* vivifies  *Nilus' slime* fertile mud left by the
Nile's annual overflow  71 *affects* choosest  *lace* i.e. of her bodice  73 *So*
provided (?) with sudden changes like my own change now (?)  *forbear*
desist  74 *stands* will sustain  75 *told* taught (through my observing how
faithful you were to her)  81 *meetly* well suited to the occasion  82 *target*
shield  84–85 *How . . . chafe* i.e. how becomingly he plays his role of angry
Hercules (from whom Antony was supposed to be descended)

Sir, you and I have loved, but there's not it:
That you know well. Something it is I would —
90 O, my oblivion is a very Antony,
And I am all forgotten.

*Antony.*                    But that your royalty
Holds idleness your subject, I should take you
For idleness itself.

*Cleopatra.*            'Tis sweating labor
To bear such idleness so near the heart
95 As Cleopatra this. But, sir, forgive me,
Since my becomings kill me when they do not
Eye well to you. Your honor calls you hence;
Therefore be deaf to my unpitied folly,
And all the gods go with you. Upon your sword
100 Sit laurel victory, and smooth success
Be strewed before your feet!

*Antony.*                    Let us go. Come:
Our separation so abides and flies
That thou residing here goes yet with me,
And I hence fleeting here remain with thee.
105 Away!                                        *Exeunt.*

I, iv    *Enter Octavius [Caesar], reading a letter, Lepidus, and*
        *their Train.*

*Caesar.* You may see, Lepidus, and henceforth know
It is not Caesar's natural vice to hate

90 *my . . . Antony* my forgetfulness is like Antony, who is now leaving, i.e. forgetting, me   91 *I . . . forgotten* (1) I have forgotten what I was going to say (2) I am all forgotten by Antony   91–92 *But . . . subject* if you were not the queen of trifling   96 *my becomings* the emotions that become me (in my situation of abandoned lover)   97 *Eye* look

Our great competitor. From Alexandria
This is the news: he fishes, drinks, and wastes
The lamps of night in revel; is not more manlike       5
Than Cleopatra, nor the queen of Ptolemy
More womanly than he; hardly gave audience, or
Vouchsafed to think he had partners. You shall find there
A man who is the abstract of all faults
That all men follow.
*Lepidus.*                    I must not think there are       10
Evils enow to darken all his goodness:
His faults, in him, seem as the spots of heaven,
More fiery by night's blackness; hereditary
Rather than purchased, what he cannot change
Than what he chooses.                                      15
*Caesar.*  You are too indulgent. Let's grant it is not
Amiss to tumble on the bed of Ptolemy,
To give a kingdom for a mirth, to sit
And keep the turn of tippling with a slave,
To reel the streets at noon, and stand the buffet       20
With knaves that smell of sweat. Say this becomes
    him
(As his composure must be rare indeed
Whom these things cannot blemish), yet must Antony
No way excuse his foils when we do bear
So great weight in his lightness. If he filled          25
His vacancy with his voluptuousness,

I, iv, 3 *competitor* partner  6 *Ptolemy* Cleopatra's dead husband  7 *audience*
i.e. to Caesar's messengers (cf. I, i)  9 *is the abstract of* sums up  11 *enow*
enough  12–13 *His . . . blackness* i.e. like stars that show the brighter by
night's blackness, Antony's faults stand out the more in the present dark
political situation  14 *purchased* acquired  19 *keep . . . of* take turns  20
*stand the buffet* trade blows  22 *his composure* that man's make-up  24 *foils*
disgraces  24–25 *when . . . lightness* when his levity puts so heavy a burden
upon us  26 *vacancy* leisure

Full surfeits and the dryness of his bones
Call on him for't. But to confound such time
That drums him from his sport and speaks as loud
30  As his own state and ours, 'tis to be chid
As we rate boys who, being mature in knowledge,
Pawn their experience to their present pleasure
And so rebel to judgment.

*Enter a Messenger.*

*Lepidus.*                     Here's more news.
*Messenger.* Thy biddings have been done, and every hour,
35  Most noble Caesar, shalt thou have report
How 'tis abroad. Pompey is strong at sea,
And it appears he is beloved of those
That only have feared Caesar: to the ports
The discontents repair, and men's reports
Give him much wronged.
40  *Caesar.*                    I should have known no less.
It hath been taught us from the primal state
That he which is was wished until he were;
And the ebbed man, ne'er loved till ne'er worth love,
Comes deared by being lacked. This common body,
45  Like to a vagabond flag upon the stream,
Goes to and back, lackeying the varying tide,
To rot itself with motion.
*Messenger.*                Caesar, I bring thee word
Menecrates and Menas, famous pirates,

*[handwritten in left margin: common wheel.]*

---

27–28 *Full . . . him* i.e. let his own physical symptoms be the reckoning  28
*confound* destroy, waste  29–30 *speaks . . . ours* calls urgently for decisions
affecting the political futures of all of us  31 *rate* berate  *mature in knowledge*
old enough to know better  33 *to judgment* against good sense  39 *discontents* discontented  40 *Give* declare  41 *from . . . state* since government
began  44 *Comes deared* becomes beloved  *common body* common people
45 *flag* iris  46 *lackeying* following obsequiously

Make the sea serve them, which they ear and wound
With keels of every kind. Many hot inroads                          50
They make in Italy; the borders maritime
Lack blood to think on't, and flush youth revolt.
No vessel can peep forth but 'tis as soon
Taken as seen; for Pompey's name strikes more
Than could his war resisted.

*Caesar.*                    Antony, *is a good soldier*
Leave thy lascivious wassails. When thou once
Was beaten from Modena, where thou slew'st
Hirtius and Pansa, consuls, at thy heel
Did famine follow, whom thou fought'st against
(Though daintily brought up) with patience more          60
Than savages could suffer. Thou didst drink
The stale of horses and the gilded puddle
Which beasts would cough at. Thy palate then did deign
The roughest berry on the rudest hedge. *alteration*
Yea, like the stag when snow the pasture sheets,          65
The barks of trees thou browsed. On the Alps *alteration*
It is reported thou didst eat strange flesh,
Which some did die to look on. And all this
(It wounds thine honor that I speak it now)
Was borne so like a soldier that thy cheek                70
So much as lanked not.

*Lepidus.*                    'Tis pity of him.

*Caesar.*  Let his shames quickly
Drive him to Rome. 'Tis time we twain
Did show ourselves i' th' field; and to that end
Assemble we immediate council. Pompey                    75
Thrives in our idleness.

*Harsh spartan life, she is firm*

52 *Lack blood* grow pale  *flush* vigorous  54–55 *strikes . . . resisted* is more
effective than his forces would be if opposed  56 *wassails* carousings  62
*stale* urine  *gilded* yellow-colored  71 *lanked* thinned

43

*Cesar and Cleopatra struggles against Antony*

*Lepidus.*              To-morrow, Caesar,
I shall be furnished to inform you rightly
Both what by sea and land I can be able
To front this present time.

*Caesar.*                 Till which encounter,
80    It is my business too. Farewell.

*Lepidus.* Farewell, my lord. What you shall know meantime
Of stirs abroad, I shall beseech you, sir,
To let me be partaker.

*Caesar.*            Doubt not, sir;
I knew it for my bond.              *Exeunt.*

I, v      *Enter Cleopatra, Charmian, Iras, and Mardian.*

*Cleopatra.* Charmian!

*Charmian.* Madam?

*Cleopatra.* Ha, ha.
Give me to drink mandragora.

*Charmian.*              Why, madam?

5 *Cleopatra.* That I might sleep out this great gap of time
My Antony is away.

*Charmian.*         You think of him too much.

*Cleopatra.* O, 'tis treason!

*Charmian.*        Madam, I trust, not so.

*Cleopatra.* Thou, eunuch Mardian!

*Mardian.*          What's your Highness' pleasure?

*Cleopatra.* Not now to hear thee sing. I take no pleasure
10    In aught an eunuch has: 'tis well for thee

78 *be able* muster   79 *front* cope with   84 *bond* duty   I, v, 3 *Ha, ha* (perhaps indicating a yawn)   4 *mandragora* mandrake (a narcotic)

That, being unseminared, thy freer thoughts
May not fly forth of Egypt. Hast thou affections?
*Mardian.* Yes, gracious madam.
*Cleopatra.* Indeed?
*Mardian.* Not in deed, madam; for I can do nothing          15
But what indeed is honest to be done:
Yet have I fierce affections, and think
What Venus did with Mars.
*Cleopatra.*                         O Charmian,
Where think'st thou he is now? Stands he, or sits he?
Or does he walk? or is he on his horse?                      20
O happy horse, to bear the weight of Antony!
Do bravely, horse! for wot'st thou whom thou mov'st?
The demi-Atlas of this earth, the arm
And burgonet of men. He's speaking now,
Or murmuring, 'Where's my serpent of old Nile?'             25
(For so he calls me). Now I feed myself
With most delicious poison. Think on me,
That am with Phoebus' amorous pinches black
And wrinkled deep in time? Broad-fronted Caesar,
When thou wast here above the ground, I was                  30
A morsel for a monarch; and great Pompey
Would stand and make his eyes grow in my brow;
There would he anchor his aspect, and die
With looking on his life.

*Enter Alexas.*

*Alexas.*                         Sovereign of Egypt, hail!
*Cleopatra.* How much unlike art thou Mark Antony!          35

11 *unseminared* unsexed  22 *wot'st* knowest  23 *demi-Atlas* i.e. Antony
and Caesar, like Atlas, support the world between them (Lepidus being of
no importance)  24 *burgonet* helmet  28 *Phoebus'* the sun's  29 *Broad-
fronted* with broad forehead  *Caesar* Julius Caesar  33 *aspect* gaze  34 S.D.
*Enter Alexas* (folio adds 'from Caesar')

45

Yet, coming from him, that great med'cine **hath**
With his tinct gilded thee.
How goes it with my brave Mark Antony?
*Alexas.* Last thing he did, dear Queen,
40  He kissed — the last of many doubled kisses —
This orient pearl. His speech sticks in my heart.
*Cleopatra.* Mine ear must pluck it thence.
*Alexas.*                          'Good friend,' quoth he,
'Say the firm Roman to great Egypt sends
This treasure of an oyster; at whose foot,
45  To mend the petty present, I will piece
Her opulent throne with kingdoms. All the East
(Say thou) shall call her mistress.' So he nodded,
And soberly did mount an arm-gaunt steed,
Who neighed so high that what I would have spoke
Was beastly dumbed by him.
50  *Cleopatra.*                  What was he, sad or merry?
*Alexas.* Like to the time o' th' year between the extremes
Of hot and cold, he was nor sad nor merry.
*Cleopatra.* O well-divided disposition! Note him,
Note him, good Charmian, 'tis the man; but note him.
55  He was not sad, for he would shine on those
That make their looks by his; he was not merry,
Which seemed to tell them his remembrance lay
In Egypt with his joy; but between both.
O heavenly mingle! Be'st thou sad or merry,
60  The violence of either thee becomes,
So does it no man else. — Met'st thou my posts?

36–37 *that* . . . *thee* (Cleopatra playfully compares Antony to the 'great medicine' of the alchemists which turned baser metals to gold: even Alexas shows some effect) 38 *brave* splendid 41 *orient* i.e. bright as the east 43 *firm* constant 48 *arm-gaunt* toughened for war (?) battle-hungry (?) 50 *dumbed* silenced 54 *the man* i.e. the real Antony 61 *posts* messengers

*Alexas.*  Ay, madam, twenty several messengers.
Why do you send so thick?
*Cleopatra.*                    Who's born that day
When I forget to send to Antony
Shall die a beggar. Ink and paper, Charmian.                    65
Welcome, my good Alexas. Did I, Charmian,
Ever love Caesar so?
*Charmian.*                O that brave Caesar!
*Cleopatra.* Be choked with such another emphasis!
Say 'the brave Antony.'
*Charmian.*                    The valiant Caesar!
*Cleopatra.* By Isis, I will give thee bloody teeth                    70
If thou with Caesar paragon again
My man of men.
*Charmian.*            By your most gracious pardon,
I sing but after you.
*Cleopatra.*              My salad days,
When I was green in judgment, cold in blood,
To say as I said then. But come, away,                    75
Get me ink and paper.
He shall have every day a several greeting,
Or I'll unpeople Egypt.                    *Exeunt.*

*Enter Pompey, Menecrates, and Menas, in warlike manner.*    II, i

*Pompey.* If the great gods be just, they shall assist
The deeds of justest men.
*Menecrates.*                    Know, worthy Pompey,
That what they do delay, they not deny.

71 *paragon* compare    73 *salad days* green youth    78 *unpeople* i.e. by send-
ing messengers to Antony

Pompey thinks 47 bad of Ant & Cleo

*Pompey.* Whiles we are suitors to their throne, decays
   The thing we sue for.
5 *Menecrates.*                      We, ignorant of ourselves,
   Beg often our own harms, which the wise pow'rs
   Deny us for our good: so find we profit
   By losing of our prayers.
*Pompey.*                         I shall do well:
   The people love me, and the sea is mine;
10   My powers are crescent, and my auguring hope
   Says it will come to th' full. Mark Antony
   In Egypt sits at dinner, and will make
   No wars without doors. Caesar gets money where
   He loses hearts. Lepidus flatters both,
15   Of both is flattered; but he neither loves,
   Nor either cares for him.
*Menas.*                        Caesar and Lepidus
   Are in the field; a mighty strength they carry.
*Pompey.* Where have you this? 'Tis false.
*Menas.*                                 From Silvius, sir.
*Pompey.* He dreams: I know they are in Rome together,
20   Looking for Antony. But all the charms of love,
   Salt Cleopatra, soften thy waned lip!
   Let witchcraft join with beauty, lust with both!
   Tie up the libertine in a field of feasts,
   Keep his brain fuming. Epicurean cooks
25   Sharpen with cloyless sauce his appetite,
   That sleep and feeding may prorogue his honor
   Even till a Lethe'd dulness —

---

II, i, 4–5 *Whiles . . . for* i.e. the thing we pray for loses its worth even while
we pray   10 *crescent* increasing   11 *it* i.e. my fortunes (imaged as a crescent
moon)   21 *Salt* lustful   *waned* faded   25 *cloyless* which never cloys
26 *prorogue* suspend   27 *Lethe'd dulness* i.e. an oblivion as deep as that which
comes from drinking of the river Lethe in the underworld

*Enter Varrius.*

       How now, Varrius?
*Varrius.* This is most certain that I shall deliver:
 Mark Antony is every hour in Rome
 Expected. Since he went from Egypt 'tis    30
 A space for farther travel.
*Pompey.*     I could have given less matter
 A better ear. Menas, I did not think
 This amorous surfeiter would have donned his helm
 For such a petty war. His soldiership
 Is twice the other twain. But let us rear    35
 The higher our opinion, that our stirring
 Can from the lap of Egypt's widow pluck
 The ne'er-lust-wearied Antony.
*Menas.*       I cannot hope
 Caesar and Antony shall well greet together;
 His wife that's dead did trespasses to Caesar;   40
 His brother warred upon him; although I think
 Not moved by Antony.
*Pompey.*     I know not, Menas,
 How lesser enmities may give way to greater.
 Were't not that we stand up against them all,
 'Twere pregnant they should square between them-
  selves,             45
 For they have entertainèd cause enough
 To draw their swords; but how the fear of us
 May cement their divisions and bind up
 The petty difference, we yet not know.

31 *A space . . . travel* time enough for even a longer journey  33 *surfeiter*
one who indulges to excess  36 *opinion* i.e. of ourselves  38 *hope* expect
39 *greet* get on  41 *brother* (cf. I, ii, 84–90)  45 *pregnant* likely  *square*
quarrel

50   Be't as our gods will have't! It only stands
     Our lives upon to use our strongest hands.
     Come, Menas.                 *Exeunt.*

*important meeting*

**II, ii**         *Enter Enobarbus and Lepidus.*

*Lepidus.* Good Enobarbus, 'tis a worthy deed,
     And shall become you well, to entreat your captain
     To soft and gentle speech.
*Enobarbus.*            I shall entreat him
     To answer like himself: if Caesar move him,
5   Let Antony look over Caesar's head
     And speak as loud as Mars. By Jupiter,
     Were I the wearer of Antonio's beard,
     I would not shave't to-day!
*Lepidus.*              'Tis not a time
     For private stomaching.
*Enobarbus.*         Every time
10   Serves for the matter that is then born in't.
*Lepidus.* But small to greater matters must give way.
*Enobarbus.* Not if the small come first.
*Lepidus.*           Your speech is passion;
     But pray you stir no embers up. Here comes
     The noble Antony.

          *Enter Antony and Ventidius.*

*Enobarbus.*         And yonder, Caesar.

50–51 *stands . . . upon* it is a matter of life and death   II, ii, 4 *like himself*
as befits his greatness   8 *I . . . shave't* i.e. I would dare Caesar to pluck it
9 *stomaching* resentment

*argument between gangsters.*

50

*Enter Caesar, Maecenas, and Agrippa.*

*Antony.* If we compose well here, to Parthia.                15
  Hark, Ventidius.
*Caesar.*                I do not know,
  Maecenas; ask Agrippa.
*Lepidus.*                    Noble friends,
  That which combined us was most great, and let not
  A leaner action rend us. What's amiss,
  May it be gently heard. When we debate        20
  Our trivial difference loud, we do commit
  Murder in healing wounds. Then, noble partners,
  The rather for I earnestly beseech,
  Touch you the sourest points with sweetest terms,
  Nor curstness grow to th' matter.
*Antony.*                          'Tis spoken well.    25
  Were we before our armies, and to fight,
  I should do thus.                          *Flourish.*
*Caesar.* Welcome to Rome.
*Antony.*                  Thank you.
*Caesar.*                      Sit.
*Antony.*                          Sit, sir.
*Caesar.*                              Nay then.
                                    *[They sit.]*

*Antony.* I learn you take things ill which are not so,
  Or being, concern you not.
*Caesar.*                      I must be laughed at    30
  If, or for nothing or a little, I
  Should say myself offended, and with you
  Chiefly i' th' world; more laughed at that I should

---

15 *compose* reach agreement   23 *The rather for* all the more because   25 *Nor
... matter* and let not ill temper make matters worse   27 *thus* (Antony makes
some courteous gesture)   31 *or ... or* either ... or

The triumvirs can create peace
& stability in Rome, but on the
contrary.

Once name you derogately, when to sound your name
It not concerned me.

35 *Antony.*              My being in Egypt, Caesar,
What was't to you?

*Caesar.* No more than my residing here at Rome
Might be to you in Egypt: yet if you there
Did practice on my state, your being in Egypt
Might be my question.

40 *Antony.*              How intend you? practiced?

*Caesar.* You may be pleased to catch at mine intent
By what did here befall me. Your wife and brother
Made wars upon me, and their contestation
Was theme for you; you were the word of war.

45 *Antony.* You do mistake your business: my brother never
Did urge me in his act. I did inquire it
And have my learning from some true reports
That drew their swords with you. Did he not rather
Discredit my authority with yours,

50 And make the wars alike against my stomach,
Having alike your cause? Of this my letters
Before did satisfy you. If you'll patch a quarrel,
As matter whole you have to make it with,
It must not be with this.

*Caesar.*              You praise yourself

55 By laying defects of judgment to me, but
You patched up your excuses.

*Antony.*              Not so, not so:
I know you could not lack, I am certain on't,

34 *derogately* disparagingly  39 *practice on* plot against  40 *question* concern
44 *you were . . . war* the war was carried on in your name  46 *urge me* use
my name  47 *reports* reporters  50 *stomach* desire  51 *Having . . . cause*
i.e. I having as much cause as you to resent it  52–54 *If . . . this* i.e. if you
are determined to patch a quarrel out of pieces, when you actually have
whole cloth to fashion it from (cf. ll. 81–98), this is not the right piece

Very necessity of this thought, that I,
Your partner in the cause 'gainst which he fought,
Could not with graceful eyes attend those wars          60
Which fronted mine own peace. As for my wife,
I would you had her spirit in such another;
The third o' th' world is yours, which with a snaffle
You may pace easy, but not such a wife.

*Enobarbus.* Would we had all such wives, that the men 65
might go to wars with the women. *Cynical*

*Antony.* So much uncurbable, her garboils, Caesar,
Made out of her impatience — which not wanted
Shrewdness of policy too — I grieving grant
Did you too much disquiet: for that you must          70
But say I could not help it.

*Caesar.*                              I wrote to you
When rioting in Alexandria; you
Did pocket up my letters, and with taunts
Did gibe my missive out of audience.

*Antony.*                              Sir,
He fell upon me, ere admitted, then:                  75
Three kings I had newly feasted, and did want
Of what I was i' th' morning; but next day
I told him of myself, which was as much
As to have asked him pardon. Let this fellow
Be nothing of our strife: if we contend,              80
Out of our question wipe him.

*Caesar.*                              You have broken
The article of your oath, which you shall never
Have tongue to charge me with.

*Lepidus.*                              Soft, Caesar.

---

60 *with ... attend* regard with pleasure   63 *snaffle* bridle bit   64 *pace* manage
67 *garboils* commotions   74 *missive* messenger   76–77 *did ... morning* was
not myself   78 *myself* my condition   81 *question* argument

*To Anthony's credit.*

*Antony.*                                        No,
    Lepidus; let him speak.
85    The honor is sacred which he talks on now,
    Supposing that I lacked it. But on, Caesar,
    The article of my oath —
*Caesar.* To lend me arms and aid when I required them,
    The which you both denied.
*Antony.*                              Neglected rather:
90    And then when poisonèd hours had bound me up
    From mine own knowledge. As nearly as I may,
    I'll play the penitent to you. But mine honesty
    Shall not make poor my greatness, nor my power
    Work without it. Truth is, that Fulvia,
95    To have me out of Egypt, made wars here,
    For which myself, the ignorant motive, do
    So far ask pardon as befits mine honor
    To stoop in such a case.
*Lepidus.*                          'Tis noble spoken.
*Maecenas.* If it might please you, to enforce no further
100    The griefs between ye: to forget them quite
    Were to remember that the present need
    Speaks to atone you.
*Lepidus.*                          Worthily spoken, Maecenas.
*Enobarbus.* Or, if you borrow one another's love for the
    instant, you may, when you hear no more words of
105    Pompey, return it again: you shall have time to wrangle
    in when you have nothing else to do.
*Antony.* Thou art a soldier only, speak no more.
*Enobarbus.* That truth should be silent I had almost forgot.

85 *honor* i.e. keeping an oath  90–91 *bound . . . knowledge* i.e. prevented my
realizing what I was doing  92–94 *mine . . . it* i.e. my actions will be
prompted by my honesty (which makes me willing to apologize) but also
by my power (which does not intend to grovel)  102 *atone* reconcile

*Antony.* You wrong this presence, therefore speak no more.

*Enobarbus.* Go to, then; your considerate stone.          110

*Caesar.* I do not much dislike the matter, but
  The manner of his speech; for't cannot be
  We shall remain in friendship, our conditions
  So diff'ring in their acts. Yet if I knew
  What hoop should hold us staunch, from edge to edge     115
  O' th' world I would pursue it.

*Agrippa.*                          Give me leave, Caesar.

*Caesar.* Speak, Agrippa.

*Agrippa.* Thou hast a sister by the mother's side,
  Admired Octavia: great Mark Antony
  Is now a widower.

*Caesar.*            Say not so, Agrippa:          120
  If Cleopatra heard you, your reproof
  Were well deserved of rashness.

*Antony.* I am not married, Caesar: let me hear
  Agrippa further speak.

*Agrippa.* To hold you in perpetual amity,          *cynical*   125
  To make you brothers, and to knit your hearts   *irony*
  With an unslipping knot, take Antony
  Octavia to his wife; whose beauty claims
  No worse a husband than the best of men;
  Whose virtue and whose general graces speak          130
  That which none else can utter. By this marriage
  All little jealousies, which now seem great,
  And all great fears, which now import their dangers,
  Would then be nothing: truths would be tales,
  Where now half-tales be truths: her love to both     135

109 *presence* company  110 *your considerate stone* i.e. I'll be dumb as a stone,
but still thinking (considering)  122 *of rashness* because of your rashness (in
ignoring Antony's bond to Cleopatra)  132 *jealousies* misunderstandings
134–35 *would be . . . be* would be taken for . . . are taken for

*Anthony is doing this in the name of honor.*

Would each to other, and all loves to both,
Draw after her. Pardon what I have spoke;
For 'tis a studied, not a present thought,
By duty ruminated.

*Antony.*               Will Caesar speak?

140 *Caesar.* Not till he hears how Antony is touched
With what is spoke already.

*Antony.*               What power is in Agrippa,
If I would say, 'Agrippa, be it so,'
To make this good?

*Caesar.*             The power of Caesar, and
His power unto Octavia.

*Antony.*             May I never

145 To this good purpose, that so fairly shows,
Dream of impediment: let me have thy hand:
Further this act of grace, and from this hour
The heart of brothers govern in our loves
And sway our great designs.

*Caesar.* _ambitious_         There is my hand.

150 A sister I bequeath you, whom no brother _Wants all._
Did ever love so dearly. Let her live _the empire_
To join our kingdoms and our hearts; and never
Fly off our loves again.

*Lepidus.*             Happily, amen.

*Antony.* I did not think to draw my sword 'gainst Pompey,

155 For he hath laid strange courtesies and great
Of late upon me. I must thank him only,
Lest my remembrance suffer ill report:
At heel of that, defy him.

*Lepidus.*             Time calls upon's.

---

145 *so fairly shows* looks so hopeful   147 *grace* reconciliation   152–53 *never
. . . loves* never may we be estranged   155 *strange* unusual   157 *remembrance*
readiness to acknowledge favors

*Good dramatic scene*

Of us must Pompey presently be sought,
Or else he seeks out us.

*Antony.*                              Where lies he?                    160
*Caesar.* About the Mount Mesena.
*Antony.* What is his strength by land?
*Caesar.* Great and increasing; but by sea
He is an absolute master.
*Antony.*                         So is the fame.
Would we had spoke together! Haste we for it,    165
Yet, ere we put ourselves in arms, dispatch we
The business we have talked of.
*Caesar.*                              With most gladness;
And do invite you to my sister's view,
Whither straight I'll lead you.
*Antony.*                         Let us, Lepidus,
Not lack your company.
*Lepidus.*                         Noble Antony,                    170
Not sickness should detain me.
                    *Flourish. [Exeunt.] Mane[n]t Enobarbus,*
                              *Agrippa, Maecenas.*

*Maecenas.* Welcome from Egypt, sir.
*Enobarbus.* Half the heart of Caesar, worthy Maecenas. My
    honorable friend, Agrippa.
*Agrippa.* Good Enobarbus.                    175
*Maecenas.* We have cause to be glad that matters are so
    well disgested. You stayed well by't in Egypt.
*Enobarbus.* Ay, sir, we did sleep day out of countenance
    and made the night light with drinking.

159 *presently* at once   161 *Mesena* i.e. Misenum, an Italian port   164 *fame*
report   171 s.d. *Exeunt* (folio reads 'Exit omnes')   173 *Half* i.e. sharing
it with Agrippa   177 *disgested* digested, arranged   *stayed . . . by't* kept at it,
'lived it up'   178–79 *we . . . drinking* i.e. we ruffled the dignity of day
(personified) by sleeping through it, and made night light (i.e. bright,
lightheaded, and wanton) with drinking parties

180 *Maecenas.* Eight wild boars roasted whole at a breakfast,
    and but twelve persons there. Is this true?
    *Enobarbus.* This was but as a fly by an eagle: we had much
    more monstrous matter of feast, which worthily deserved
    noting.
185 *Maecenas.* She's a most triumphant lady, if report be square
    to her.
    *Enobarbus.* When she first met Mark Antony, she pursed
    up his heart, upon the river of Cydnus.
    *Agrippa.* There she appeared indeed; or my reporter de-
190 vised well for her.
    *Enobarbus.* I will tell you. *all paradox is*
    The barge she sat in, like a burnished throne,
    Burned on the water: the poop was beaten gold;
    Purple the sails, and so perfumèd that
195 The winds were lovesick with them; the oars were silver,
    Which to the tune of flutes kept stroke, and made
    The water which they beat to follow faster,
    As amorous of their strokes. For her own person,
    It beggared all description: she did lie
200 In her pavilion, cloth-of-gold of tissue,
    O'erpicturing that Venus where we see
    The fancy outwork nature. On each side her
    Stood pretty dimpled boys, like smiling Cupids,
    With divers-colored fans, whose wind did seem
205 To glow the delicate cheeks which they did cool,
    And what they undid did.
    *Agrippa.*                    O, rare for Antony.

---

**182** *by* compared to   **185** *square* fair   **187–88** *pursed up* pocketed (but with
a suggestion of pursed lips for kissing)   **189** *appeared* came before the public
**189–90** *devised* invented   **200** *cloth-of-gold of tissue* cloth interwoven with
gold threads   **201** *O'er-picturing* outdoing the picture of   **202** *fancy* i.e. the
painter's imagination   **205** *glow* make glow (as if heated)

*Good description - unnatural - very complimentary*

*Enobarbus.* Her gentlewomen, like the Nereides,
   So many mermaids, tended her i' th' eyes,
   And made their bends adornings. At the helm
   A seeming mermaid steers: the silken tackle                210
   Swell with the touches of those flower-soft hands,
   That yarely frame the office. From the barge
   A strange invisible perfume hits the sense
   Of the adjacent wharfs. The city cast
   Her people out upon her; and Antony,                        215
   Enthroned i' th' market place, did sit alone,
   Whistling to th' air; which, but for vacancy,
   Had gone to gaze on Cleopatra too,
   And made a gap in nature.
*Agrippa.*               Rare Egyptian!
*Enobarbus.* Upon her landing, Antony sent to her,              220
   Invited her to supper. She replied,
   It should be better he became her guest;
   Which she entreated. Our courteous Antony, *ladyman*
   Whom ne'er the word of 'no' woman heard speak,
   Being barbered ten times o'er, goes to the feast,          225
   And for his ordinary pays his heart
   For what his eyes eat only.
*Agrippa.*             Royal wench!
   She made great Caesar lay his sword to bed;
   He ploughed her, and she cropped.
*Enobarbus.*           I saw her once
   Hop forty paces through the public street;                 230
   And having lost her breath, she spoke, and panted,

207 *Nereides* sea nymphs  208 *tended . . . eyes* waited on her every glance
209 *made . . . adornings* made their postures of submission decorative (as in
a tableau)  212 *yarely frame* nimbly perform  217 *but for vacancy* except
that it would have left a vacuum  226 *ordinary* meal  229 *cropped* bore fruit
(i.e. Julius Caesar's son, Caesarion)

That she did make defect perfection
And, breathless, pow'r breathe forth.

*Maecenas.* Now Antony must leave her utterly.

235 *Enobarbus.* Never; he will not:
Age cannot wither her, nor custom stale
Her infinite variety: other women cloy
The appetites they feed, but she makes hungry
Where most she satisfies. For vilest things
240 Become themselves in her, that the holy priests
Bless her when she is riggish.

*Maecenas.* If beauty, wisdom, modesty, can settle
The heart of Antony, Octavia is
A blessèd lottery to him.

*Agrippa.*             Let us go.

245 Good Enobarbus, make yourself my guest
Whilst you abide here.

*Enobarbus.*         Humbly, sir, I thank you. *Exeunt.*

❊

II, iii      *Enter Antony, Caesar, Octavia between them.*

*Antony.* The world and my great office will sometimes
Divide me from your bosom.

*Octavia.*               All which time
Before the gods my knee shall bow my prayers
To them for you.

*Antony.*        Good night, sir. My Octavia,
5 Read not my blemishes in the world's report:
I have not kept my square, but that to come
Shall all be done by th' rule. Good night, dear lady

---

232 *defect* i.e. the resulting breathlessness   240 *Become . . . her* are so becoming to her   241 *riggish* lewd   244 *lottery* gift of fortune   II, iii, 6 *square* carpenter's square (i.e. I have not followed the straight and narrow)

*Octavia.* Good night, sir.
*Caesar.* Good night.                    *Exit [with Octavia].*

*Enter Soothsayer.*

*Antony.* Now, sirrah: you do wish yourself in Egypt?    10
*Soothsayer.* Would I had never come from thence, nor you
  thither.
*Antony.* If you can, your reason?
*Soothsayer.* I see it in my motion, have it not in my tongue,
  But yet hie you to Egypt again.
*Antony.*                    Say to me,    15
  Whose fortunes shall rise higher, Caesar's or mine?
*Soothsayer.* Caesar's.
  Therefore, O Antony, stay not by his side.
  Thy demon, that thy spirit which keeps thee, is
  Noble, courageous, high, unmatchable,    20
  Where Caesar's is not. But near him thy angel
  Becomes a fear, as being o'erpow'red. Therefore
  Make space enough between you.
*Antony.*                    Speak this no more.
*Soothsayer.* To none but thee, no more but when to thee.
  If thou dost play with him at any game,    25
  Thou art sure to lose; and of that natural luck
  He beats thee 'gainst the odds. Thy lustre thickens
  When he shines by: I say again, thy spirit
  Is all afraid to govern thee near him;
  But he away, 'tis noble.
*Antony.*                    Get thee gone.    30
  Say to Ventidius I would speak with him.
                    *Exit [Soothsayer].*
  He shall to Parthia. — Be it art or hap,

14 *motion* mind   19 *demon* guardian angel   22 *a fear* i.e. timorous   27
*thickens* dims   32 *art or hap* skill or chance

61

Anthony is not interested in
success or fortune.

He hath spoken true. The very dice obey him,
And in our sports my better cunning faints
35 Under his chance: if we draw lots, he speeds;
His cocks do win the battle still of mine
When it is all to naught, and his quails ever
Beat mine, inhooped, at odds. I will to Egypt:
And though I make this marriage for my peace,
I' th' East my pleasure lies.

*Enter Ventidius.*

40                           O, come, Ventidius,
You must to Parthia. Your commission 's ready:
Follow me, and receive't.                    *Exeunt.*

II, iv          *Enter Lepidus, Maecenas, and Agrippa.*

*Lepidus.* Trouble yourselves no further: pray you, hasten
    Your generals after.
*Agrippa.*               Sir, Mark Antony
    Will e'en but kiss Octavia, and we'll follow.
*Lepidus.* Till I shall see you in your soldier's dress,
    Which will become you both, farewell.
5 *Maecenas.*                        We shall,
    As I conceive the journey, be at Mount
    Before you, Lepidus.
*Lepidus.*           Your way is shorter;
    My purposes do draw me much about:
    You'll win two days upon me.

34 *cunning* skill  35 *chance* luck  *speeds* wins  36 *still* always  37 *it* . . .
*naught* i.e. the odds are everything to nothing in my favor  38 *inhooped*
i.e. fighting confined within a hoop  II, iv, 6 *Mount* (cf. II, ii, 161)  8 *about*
roundabout

*Both.*                              Sir, good success.
*Lepidus.* Farewell.                              *Exeunt.* 10

    *Enter Cleopatra, Charmian, Iras, and Alexas.*        II, v
*Cleopatra.* Give me some music: music, moody food
  Of us that trade in love.
*Omnes.*                              The music, ho!

    *Enter Mardian the Eunuch.*

*Cleopatra.* Let it alone, let's to billiards: come, Charmian.
*Charmian.* My arm is sore; best play with Mardian.
*Cleopatra.* As well a woman with an eunuch played        5
  As with a woman. Come, you'll play with me, sir?
*Mardian.* As well as I can, madam.
*Cleopatra.* And when good will is showed, though't come
    too short,
  The actor may plead pardon. I'll none now.
  Give me mine angle, we'll to th' river: there,        10
  My music playing far off, I will betray
  Tawny-finned fishes. My bended hook shall pierce
  Their slimy jaws; and as I draw them up,
  I'll think them every one an Antony,
  And say, 'Ah, ha! y' are caught!'
*Charmian.*                              'Twas merry when        15
  You wagered on your angling, when your diver
  Did hang a salt fish on his hook, which he
  With fervency drew up.
*Cleopatra.*                              That time — O times! —
  I laughed him out of patience; and that night

II, v, 10 *angle* fishing tackle   17 *salt* dried

20 I laughed him into patience; and next morn
    Ere the ninth hour I drunk him to his bed;
    Then put my tires and mantles on him, whilst
    I wore his sword Philippan.

*Enter a Messenger.*

                     O, from Italy!
    Ram thou thy fruitful tidings in mine ears,
    That long time have been barren.
25 *Messenger.*                 Madam, madam —
    *Cleopatra.* Antonio's dead: if thou say so, villain,
    Thou kill'st thy mistress: but well and free,
    If thou so yield him, there is gold and here
    My bluest veins to kiss, a hand that kings
30 Have lipped, and trembled kissing.
    *Messenger.* First, madam, he is well.
    *Cleopatra.*               Why, there's more gold.
    But, sirrah, mark, we use
    To say the dead are well: bring it to that,
    The gold I give thee will I melt and pour
35 Down thy ill-uttering throat.
    *Messenger.* Good madam, hear me.
    *Cleopatra.*              Well, go to, I will:
    But there's no goodness in thy face if Antony
    Be free and healthful; so tart a favor
    To trumpet such good tidings? If not well,
40 Thou shouldst come like a Fury crowned with snakes,
    Not like a formal man.
    *Messenger.*            Will't please you hear me?

22 *tires* headdresses   23 *Philippan* (so called because he had beaten Brutus
and Cassius with it at Philippi)   33 *well* i.e. in heaven   *bring . . . that* say
that you mean that   37 *goodness* i.e. truth   38 *tart a favor* sour a face   41 *Not
. . . man* not in human shape

*She is acting like a natural force.*

*Cleopatra.* I have a mind to strike thee ere thou speak'st:
  Yet, if thou say Antony lives, is well,
  Or friends with Caesar, or not captive to him,
  I'll set thee in a shower of gold, and hail                    45
  Rich pearls upon thee.
*Messenger.*                    Madam, he's well.
*Cleopatra.*                                        Well said.
*Messenger.* And friends with Caesar.
*Cleopatra.*                                Th' art an honest man.
*Messenger.* Caesar and he are greater friends than ever.
*Cleopatra.* Make thee a fortune from me.
*Messenger.*                                But yet, madam —
*Cleopatra.* I do not like 'but yet,' it does allay              50
  The good precedence: fie upon 'but yet,'
  'But yet' is as a jailer to bring forth
  Some monstrous malefactor. Prithee, friend,
  Pour out the pack of matter to mine ear,
  The good and bad together: he's friends with Caesar,    55
  In state of health, thou say'st, and thou say'st, free.
*Messenger.* Free, madam, no: I made no such report,
  He's bound unto Octavia.
*Cleopatra.*                    For what good turn?
*Messenger.* For the best turn i' th' bed.
*Cleopatra.*                        I am pale, Charmian.
*Messenger.* Madam, he's married to Octavia.                    60
*Cleopatra.* The most infectious pestilence upon thee!
                                        *Strikes him down.*
*Messenger.* Good madam, patience.
*Cleopatra.*                            What say you?
                                            *Strikes him.*
                                            Hence,
  Horrible villain! or I'll spurn thine eyes

50–51 *allay . . . precedence* spoil the good that preceded it   63 *spurn* kick

*Cleopatra tantrum, indicates her love for Antony.*

65

Like balls before me: I'll unhair thy head,

               *She hales him up and down.*

65 Thou shalt be whipped with wire and stewed in brine,
    Smarting in ling'ring pickle.

*Messenger.*                Gracious madam,
    I that do bring the news made not the match.

*Cleopatra.* Say 'tis not so, a province I will give thee,
    And make thy fortunes proud: the blow thou hadst
70 Shall make thy peace for moving me to rage,
    And I will boot thee with what gift beside
    Thy modesty can beg.

*Messenger.*          He's married, madam.

*Cleopatra.* Rogue, thou hast lived too long.    *Draw a knife.*

*Messenger.*               Nay, then I'll run.
    What mean you, madam? I have made no fault.    *Exit.*

75 *Charmian.* Good madam, keep yourself within yourself,
    The man is innocent.

*Cleopatra.* Some innocents 'scape not the thunderbolt.
    Melt Egypt into Nile! and kindly creatures
    Turn all to serpents! Call the slave again:
80 Though I am mad, I will not bite him. Call!

*Charmian.* He is afeard to come.

*Cleopatra.*            I will not hurt him.

                     *[Exit Charmian.]*

These hands do lack nobility, that they strike
A meaner than myself; since I myself
Have given myself the cause.

      *Enter [Charmian and] the Messenger again.*

                  Come hither, sir.
85 Though it be honest, it is never good

---

64 s.d. *hales* drags   66 *pickle* pickling solution   71 *boot* benefit   72 *modesty*
humble condition   84 *cause* i.e. by loving Antony

To bring bad news: give to a gracious message
An host of tongues, but let ill tidings tell
Themselves when they be felt.

*Messenger.* I have done my duty.

*Cleopatra.* Is he married?
I cannot hate thee worser than I do                                    90
If thou again say 'Yes.'

*Messenger.* He's married, madam.

*Cleopatra.* The gods confound thee! Dost thou hold there
still?

*Messenger.* Should I lie, madam?

*Cleopatra.* O, I would thou didst,
So half my Egypt were submerged and made
A cistern for scaled snakes! Go get thee hence;                        95
Hadst thou Narcissus in thy face, to me
Thou wouldst appear most ugly. He is married?

*Messenger.* I crave your Highness' pardon.

*Cleopatra.* He is married?

*Messenger.* Take no offense that I would not offend you:
To punish me for what you make me do                                  100
Seems much unequal: he's married to Octavia.

*Cleopatra.* O, that his fault should make a knave of thee,
That art not what th' art sure of! Get thee hence,
The merchandise which thou hast brought from Rome
Are all too dear for me. Lie they upon thy hand,                      105
And be undone by 'em!                    *[Exit Messenger.]*

*Charmian.* Good your Highness, patience.

*Cleopatra.* In praising Antony I have dispraised Caesar.

92 *confound* destroy   94 *So* even though   96 *Hadst . . . face* were you as
handsome as Narcissus (in Greek legend, the youth who fell in love with his
image reflected in a stream)   99 *Take . . . you* don't be angry that I'd rather
not anger you (i.e. by answering)   101 *unequal* unjust   103 *That . . . of* i.e.
who are not really hateful, like the news you bring   105 *upon thy hand* i.e.
unsold   106 *undone* bankrupt

*Charmian.* Many times, madam.

*Cleopatra.*                    I am paid for't now.
Lead me from hence,
110 I faint. O Iras, Charmian! 'Tis no matter.
Go to the fellow, good Alexas; bid him
Report the feature of Octavia: her years,
Her inclination, let him not leave out
The color of her hair. Bring me word quickly.

                                    *[Exit Alexas.]*

115 Let him for ever go! — let him not! — Charmian,
Though he be painted one way like a Gorgon,
The other way 's a Mars. *[to Mardian]* Bid you Alexas
Bring me word how tall she is. — Pity me, Charmian,
But do not speak to me. Lead me to my chamber. *Exeunt.*

II, vi     *Flourish. Enter Pompey at one door, with Drum and
           Trumpet: at another, Caesar, Lepidus, Antony, Eno-
           barbus, Maecenas, Agrippa, Menas, with Soldiers
           marching.*

*Pompey.* Your hostages I have, so have you mine;
And we shall talk before we fight.

*Caesar.*                              Most meet
That first we come to words, and therefore have we
Our written purposes before us sent;
5   Which if thou hast considerèd, let us know
If 'twill tie up thy discontented sword
And carry back to Sicily much tall youth
That else must perish here.

116 *Gorgon* Medusa (the sight of whose ugly face turned men to stone)
II, vi, 2 *meet* suitable   7 *tall* bold

*Pompey.*                         To you all three,
The senators alone of this great world,
Chief factors for the gods: I do not know                    10
Wherefore my father should revengers want,
Having a son and friends, since Julius Caesar,
Who at Philippi the good Brutus ghosted,
There saw you laboring for him. What was't
That moved pale Cassius to conspire? And what          15
Made all-honored, honest, Roman Brutus,
With the armed rest, courtiers of beauteous freedom,
To drench the Capitol, but that they would
Have one man but a man? And that is it
Hath made me rig my navy, at whose burden              20
The angered ocean foams; with which I meant
To scourge th' ingratitude that despiteful Rome
Cast on my noble father.

*Caesar.*                         Take your time.

*Antony.* Thou canst not fear us, Pompey, with thy sails.
We'll speak with thee at sea. At land thou know'st      25
How much we do o'ercount thee.

*Pompey.*                         At land indeed
Thou dost o'ercount me of my father's house:
But since the cuckoo builds not for himself,
Remain in't as thou mayst.

*Lepidus.*                         Be pleased to tell us
(For this is from the present) how you take               30
The offers we have sent you.

*Caesar.*                         There's the point.

---

10 *factors* agents   13 *ghosted* haunted   24 *fear* frighten   25 *speak* contest
26 *o'ercount* outnumber   27 *o'ercount* cheat   *house* (Plutarch says that
Antony had bought this house but not paid for it)   28 *cuckoo* (which never
builds its own nest but lays its eggs in the nests of other birds)   29 *as thou
mayst* as long as you can   30 *from the present* off the topic

*Antony.* Which do not be entreated to, but weigh
    What it is worth embraced.

*Caesar.*                         And what may follow,
    To try a larger fortune.

*Pompey.*                     You have made me offer
35   Of Sicily, Sardinia; and I must
    Rid all the sea of pirates; then, to send
    Measures of wheat to Rome; this 'greed upon,
    To part with unhacked edges and bear back
    Our targes undinted.

*Omnes.*                 That's our offer.

*Pompey.*                             Know then
40   I came before you here a man prepared
    To take this offer; but Mark Antony
    Put me to some impatience. Though I lose
    The praise of it by telling, you must know,
    When Caesar and your brother were at blows,
45   Your mother came to Sicily and did find
    Her welcome friendly.

*Antony.*                     I have heard it, Pompey,
    And am well studied for a liberal thanks,
    Which I do owe you.

*Pompey.*                   Let me have your hand:
    I did not think, sir, to have met you here.

*Antony.* The beds i' th' East are soft; and thanks to
50   you,
    That called me timelier than my purpose hither;
    For I have gained by't.

*Caesar.*                       Since I saw you last
    There's a change upon you.

---

33 *embraced* if accepted  34 *a larger fortune* i.e. war with the triumvirs  38
*edges* swords  39 *targes* shields  *Omnes* all (Antony, Caesar, Lepidus)
47 *studied for* prepared with

*Pompey.*                    Well, I know not
  What counts harsh fortune casts upon my face,
  But in my bosom shall she never come                    55
  To make my heart her vassal.
*Lepidus.*                    Well met here.
*Pompey.* I hope so, Lepidus. Thus we are agreed.
  I crave our composition may be written,
  And sealed between us.
*Caesar.*                    That's the next to do.
*Pompey.* We'll feast each other ere we part, and let's    60
  Draw lots who shall begin.
*Antony.*                    That will I, Pompey.
*Pompey.* No, Antony, take the lot:
  But, first or last, your fine Egyptian cookery
  Shall have the fame. I have heard that Julius Caesar
  Grew fat with feasting there.
*Antony.*                    You have heard much.    65
*Pompey.* I have fair meanings, sir.
*Antony.*                    And fair words to them.
*Pompey.* Then so much have I heard,
  And I have heard Apollodorus carried —
*Enobarbus.* No more of that: he did so.
*Pompey.*                    What, I pray you?
*Enobarbus.* A certain queen to Caesar in a mattress.    70
*Pompey.* I know thee now; how far'st thou, soldier?
*Enobarbus.*                    Well;
  And well am like to do, for I perceive
  Four feasts are toward.
*Pompey.*                    Let me shake thy hand,
  I never hated thee: I have seen thee fight
  When I have envied thy behavior.

54 *counts* tallies (as on a scoring stick)   58 *composition* agreement   73
*toward* coming up

75 *Enobarbus.*                                    Sir,
    I never loved you much; but I ha' praised ye
    When you have well deserved ten times as much
    As I have said you did.
    *Pompey.*                        Enjoy thy plainness,
    It nothing ill becomes thee.
80  Aboard my galley I invite you all:
    Will you lead, lords?
    *All.*                          Show 's the way, sir.
    *Pompey.*                                        Come.
                    *Exeunt. Mane[n]t Enobarbus and Menas.*
    *Menas. [aside]* Thy father, Pompey, would ne'er have
    made this treaty. — You and I have known, sir.
    *Enobarbus.* At sea, I think.
85  *Menas.* We have, sir.
    *Enobarbus.* You have done well by water.
    *Menas.* And you by land.
    *Enobarbus.* I will praise any man that will praise me;
    though it cannot be denied what I have done by land.
90  *Menas.* Nor what I have done by water.
    *Enobarbus.* Yes, something you can deny for your own
    safety: you have been a great thief by sea.
    *Menas.* And you by land.
    *Enobarbus.* There I deny my land service. But give me
95  your hand, Menas: if our eyes had authority, here they
    might take two thieves kissing.
    *Menas.* All men's faces are true, whatsome'er their hands
    are.
    *Enobarbus.* But there is never a fair woman has a true face.
100 *Menas.* No slander, they steal hearts.
    *Enobarbus.* We came hither to fight with you.

79 *nothing* not at all   83 *known* met   95 *had* were in   99 *true* honest

*Menas.* For my part, I am sorry it is turned to a drinking.
Pompey doth this day laugh away his fortune.

*Enobarbus.* If he do, sure he cannot weep't back again.

*Menas.* Y' have said, sir. We looked not for Mark Antony   105
here. Pray you, is he married to Cleopatra?

*Enobarbus.* Caesar's sister is called Octavia.

*Menas.* True, sir, she was the wife of Caius Marcellus.

*Enobarbus.* But she is now the wife of Marcus Antonius.

*Menas.* Pray ye, sir?                                        110

*Enobarbus.* 'Tis true.

*Menas.* Then is Caesar and he for ever knit together.

*Enobarbus.* If I were bound to divine of this unity, I would
not prophesy so.

*Menas.* I think the policy of that purpose made more in the  115
marriage than the love of the parties.

*Enobarbus.* I think so too. But you shall find the band that
sccms to tie their friendship together will be the very
strangler of their amity: Octavia is of a holy, cold, and
still conversation.                                          120

*Menas.* Who would not have his wife so?

*Enobarbus.* Not he that himself is not so; which is Mark
Antony. He will to his Egyptian dish again: then shall
the sighs of Octavia blow the fire up in Caesar, and, as I
said before, that which is the strength of their amity shall  125
prove the immediate author of their variance. Antony
will use his affection where it is. He married but his
occasion here.

*Menas.* And thus it may be. Come, sir, will you aboard?
I have a health for you.                                     130

---

105 *Y' have said* i.e. you are quite right   110 *Pray ye* i.e. how's that again
115 *made more* played more part   120 *conversation* way of life   127 *where it
is* i.e. in Egypt   128 *occasion* convenience

*Enobarbus.* I shall take it, sir: we have used our throats in
Egypt.

*Menas.* Come, let's away. *Exeunt.*

*[handwritten: Feast: political celebration — a drum ben drawl.]*

II, vii   *Music plays. Enter two or three Servants, with a banquet.*

1. *[Servant].* Here they'll be, man. Some o' their plants
are ill-rooted already; the least wind i' th' world will
blow them down.

2. *[Servant].* Lepidus is high-colored.

5  1. *[Servant].* They have made him drink alms-drink.

2. *[Servant].* As they pinch one another by the disposition,
he cries out 'No more,' reconciles them to his entreaty,
and himself to th' drink.

1. *[Servant].* But it raises the greater war between him and
10  his discretion.

2. *[Servant].* Why, this it is to have a name in great men's
fellowship. I had as live have a reed that will do me no
service as a partisan I could not heave.

1. *[Servant].* To be called into a huge sphere and not to be
15  seen to move in't, are the holes where eyes should be,
which pitifully disaster the cheeks.

---

II, vii, 1 *plants* feet (with pun on the usual sense: cf. 'ill-rooted') 5 *alms-
drink* drink drunk on behalf of one too far gone to continue his part in a
round of toasts (Lepidus has been tricked into drinking more than the rest)
7 *No more* i.e. no more quarrelling 12 *live* lief 13 *partisan* spear 14–16 *To
. . . cheeks* (Lepidus, a little man in a part too big for him, is compared first
to a heavenly body that fails to perform its function in its *sphere,* and then
to a face without eyes; *disaster,* carrying the image back on itself, likens
the face without eyes to a heaven without stars)

*A sennet sounded. Enter Caesar, Antony, Pompey,
Lepidus, Agrippa, Maecenas, Enobarbus, Menas, with
other Captains.*

*Antony.* Thus do they, sir: they take the flow o' th'
  Nile *similar to the feast in Egypt*
By certain scales i' th' pyramid. They know
By th' height, the lowness, or the mean, if dearth
Or foison follow. The higher Nilus swells,                    20
The more it promises; as it ebbs, the seedsman
Upon the slime and ooze scatters his grain,
And shortly comes to harvest.
*Lepidus.* Y' have strange serpents there.
*Antony.* Ay, Lepidus.                                        25
*Lepidus.* Your serpent of Egypt is bred now of your mud
  by the operation of your sun: so is your crocodile.
*Antony.* They are so.
*Pompey.* Sit — and some wine! A health to Lepidus!
*Lepidus.* I am not so well as I should be, but I'll ne'er out. 30
*Enobarbus.* Not till you have slept. I fear me you'll be in
  till then.
*Lepidus.* Nay, certainly, I have heard the Ptolemies' pyra-
  mises are very goodly things: without contradiction I
  have heard that.                                            35
*Menas.* Pompey, a word.
*Pompey.*                    Say in mine ear. What is't?
*Menas.* Forsake thy seat, I do beseech thee, captain,
And hear me speak a word.

---

16 S.D. *sennet* distinctive set of trumpet notes announcing persons of importance    18 *scales* graduations    19–20 *dearth Or foison* famine or plenty
30 *ne'er out* never give up    31 *in* drunk    33–34 *pyramises* (Lepidus's
drunken rendering of 'pyramides,' i.e. pyramids)

*Pompey.*                 Forbear me till anon.

                          *[Menas] whispers in's ear.*

    This wine for Lepidus!

40 *Lepidus.* What manner o' thing is your crocodile?

*Antony.* It is shaped, sir, like itself, and it is as broad as it
    hath breadth; it is just so high as it is, and moves with it
    own organs. It lives by that which nourisheth it, and
    the elements once out of it, it transmigrates.

45 *Lepidus.* What color is it of?

*Antony.* Of it own color too.

*Lepidus.* 'Tis a strange serpent.

*Antony.* 'Tis so, and the tears of it are wet.

*Caesar.* Will this description satisfy him?

50 *Antony.* With the health that Pompey gives him; else he
    is a very epicure.

                          *[Menas whispers again.]*

*Pompey.* Go hang, sir, hang! Tell me of that? Away!
    Do as I bid you. — Where's this cup I called for?

*Menas.* If for the sake of merit thou wilt hear me,
    Rise from thy stool.

*Pompey.*           I think th'art mad.

                       *[Rises and walks aside.]*

55                       The matter?

*Menas.* I have ever held my cap off to thy fortunes.

*Pompey.* Thou hast served me with much faith. What's
    else to say? —

    Be jolly, lords.

*Antony.*         These quicksands, Lepidus,
    Keep off them, for you sink.

*Menas.* Wilt thou be lord of all the world?

---

42–43, 46 *it own* its own    44 *transmigrates* i.e. its soul takes over the body
of some other creature (Antony is teasing the drunken Lepidus)    48 *tears*
i.e. its 'crocodile tears'    56 *held . . . off* i.e. been devoted

*Celebration of peace. It is a resolution-*

*Pompey.*                                What say'st thou?      60
*Menas.* Wilt thou be lord of the whole world? That's twice.
*Pompey.* How should that be?
*Menas.*                           But entertain it,
   And though thou think me poor, I am the man
   Will give thee all the world.
*Pompey.*                         Hast thou drunk well?
*Menas.* No, Pompey, I have kept me from the cup.      65
   Thou art, if thou dar'st be, the earthly Jove:
   Whate'er the ocean pales, or sky inclips,
   Is thine, if thou wilt ha't.
*Pompey.*                      Show me which way.
*Menas.* These three world-sharers, these competitors,
   Are in thy vessel. Let me cut the cable;            70
   And when we are put off, fall to their throats.
   All there is thine.
*Pompey.*           Ah, this thou shouldst have done,
   And not have spoke on't. In me 'tis villainy,
   In thee 't had been good service. Thou must know,
   'Tis not my profit that does lead mine honor;       75
   Mine honor, it. Repent that e'er thy tongue
   Hath so betrayed thine act. Being done unknown,
   I should have found it afterwards well done,
   But must condemn it now. Desist, and drink.
*Menas.* [*aside*] For this,
   I'll never follow thy palled fortunes more.
   Who seeks, and will not take when once 'tis offered,
   Shall never find it more.
*Pompey.*                   This health to Lepidus!
*Antony.* Bear him ashore. I'll pledge it for him, Pompey.

62 *But entertain it* only accept the idea   67 *pales* encloses   69 *competitors*
partners   76 *Mine honor, it* i.e. my honor comes before my profit   81 *palled*
decayed   84 *I'll . . . him* (cf. l. 5: Antony is now taking an 'alms-drink')

*Momentary peace for Antony.*

*Enobarbus.* Here's to thee, Menas.

85 *Menas.*                              Enobarbus, welcome.

*Pompey.* Fill till the cup be hid.

*Enobarbus.* There's a strong fellow, Menas.

> [*Points to the Servant who carries off Lepidus.*]

*Menas.* Why?

*Enobarbus.* 'A bears the third part of the world, man;
90     seest not?

*Menas.* The third part then is drunk. Would it were all,
    That it might go on wheels!

*Enobarbus.* Drink thou: increase the reels.

*Menas.* Come.

95 *Pompey.* This is not yet an Alexandrian feast.

*Antony.* It ripens towards it. Strike the vessels, ho!
    Here's to Caesar!

*Caesar.*                  I could well forbear't.
    It's monstrous labor when I wash my brain
    And it grows fouler.

*Antony.*                  Be a child o' th' time.

100 *Caesar.* Possess it, I'll make answer;
    But I had rather fast from all four days
    Than drink so much in one.

*Enobarbus.*                          Ha, my brave emperor!
    Shall we dance now the Egyptian Bacchanals
    And celebrate our drink?

*Pompey.*                  Let's ha't, good soldier.

105 *Antony.* Come, let's all take hands
    Till that the conquering wine hath steeped our sense
    In soft and delicate Lethe.

*Enobarbus.*                  All take hands:
    Make battery to our ears with the loud music;

---

92 *go on wheels* whirl smoothly   93 *reels* whirls   96 *Strike the vessels*
broach the casks   97 *forbear't* i.e. pass up this toast   100 *Possess it* down it
107 *Lethe* (cf. II, i, 27n.)

*Dramatic presentatis*

The while I'll place you; then the boy shall sing.
The holding every man shall bear as loud                110
As his strong sides can volley.

*Music plays. Enobarbus places them hand in hand.*

### The Song.

Come, thou monarch of the vine,
Plumpy Bacchus with pink eyne!
In thy fats our cares be drowned,
With thy grapes our hairs be crowned.             115
  Cup us till the world go round,
  Cup us till the world go round!

*Caesar.* What would you more? Pompey, good night.
  Good brother,
Let me request you off: our graver business
Frowns at this levity. Gentle lords, let's part;          120
You see we have burnt our cheeks. Strong Enobarb
Is weaker than the wine, and mine own tongue
Splits what it speaks: the wild disguise hath almost
Anticked us all. What needs more words? Good night.
Good Antony, your hand.
*Pompey.*                         I'll try you on the shore.      125
*Antony.* And shall, sir. — Give's your hand.
*Pompey.*                                    O Antony,
You have my father's house. But what, we are friends!
Come down into the boat.
*Enobarbus.*                   Take heed you fall not.
                *[Exeunt all but Enobarbus and Menas.]*
Menas, I'll not on shore.

---

110 *holding* refrain   113 *pink* half-closed   114 *fats* vats   119 *off* to come
away   123 *disguise* dancing and drinking   124 *Anticked* made fools of
125 *try you* take you on in a drinking bout

79

*Menas.*                              No, to my cabin.
130    These drums! these trumpets, flutes! what!
       Let Neptune hear we bid a loud farewell
       To these great fellows. Sound and be hanged, sound out!
                                   *Sound a flourish, with drums.*
       *Enobarbus.* Hoo! says 'a. There's my cap.
       *Menas.* Hoa! Noble captain, come.                    *Exeunt.*

III, i    *Enter Ventidius as it were in triumph, the dead body of*
          *Pacorus borne before him [by Romans].*

*Ventidius.* Now, darting Parthia, art thou struck, and now
       Pleased fortune does of Marcus Crassus' death
       Make me revenger. Bear the King's son's body
       Before our army. Thy Pacorus, Orodes,
       Pays this for Marcus Crassus.
5  *Roman [Silius].*                       Noble Ventidius,
       Whilst yet with Parthian blood thy sword is warm,
       The fugitive Parthians follow. Spur through Media,
       Mesopotamia, and the shelters whither
       The routed fly: so thy grand captain, Antony,
10     Shall set thee on triumphant chariots and
       Put garlands on thy head.
*Ventidius.*                       O Silius, Silius,
       I have done enough. A lower place, note well,
       May make too great an act. For learn this, Silius,
       Better to leave undone, than by our deed

III, i, 1 *darting* i.e. famous for its bowmen   5 *Marcus Crassus* (member of
the first triumvirate with Pompey the Great and Julius Caesar, who was
killed by the Parthians and who is now avenged by the death of Pacorus,
son to Orodes the Parthian king)   12 *A lower place* an underling

Acquire too high a fame when him we serve's away.        15
Caesar and Antony have ever won
More in their officer than person. Sossius,
One of my place in Syria, his lieutenant,
For quick accumulation of renown,
Which he achieved by th' minute, lost his favor.        20
Who does i' th' wars more than his captain can
Becomes his captain's captain; and ambition
(The soldier's virtue) rather makes choice of loss
Than gain which darkens him.
I could do more to do Antonius good,        25
But 'twould offend him. And in his offense
Should my performance perish.
*Roman [Silius].*            Thou hast, Ventidius, that
Without the which a soldier and his sword
Grants scarce distinction. Thou wilt write to Antony?
*Ventidius.* I'll humbly signify what in his name,        30
That magical word of war, we have effected;
How with his banners and his well-paid ranks
The ne'er-yet-beaten horse of Parthia
We have jaded out o' th' field.
*Roman [Silius].*            Where is he now?
*Ventidius.* He purposeth to Athens; whither, with what
        haste        35
The weight we must convey with's will permit,
We shall appear before him. — On, there, pass along.
                                    *Exeunt.*

---

26 *in his offense* in offending him    27 *that* i.e. discretion    34 *jaded* driven
weary

*Enter Agrippa at one door, Enobarbus at another.*

*Agrippa.* What, are the brothers parted?
*Enobarbus.* They have dispatched with Pompey; he is gone;
The other three are sealing. Octavia weeps
To part from Rome; Caesar is sad, and Lepidus
5 Since Pompey's feast, as Menas says, is troubled
With the green-sickness.
*Agrippa.* 'Tis a noble Lepidus.
*Enobarbus.* A very fine one. O, how he loves Caesar!
*Agrippa.* Nay, but how dearly he adores Mark Antony!
*Enobarbus.* Caesar? Why, he's the Jupiter of men.
10 *Agrippa.* What's Antony? The god of Jupiter.
*Enobarbus.* Spake you of Caesar? How! the nonpareil!
*Agrippa.* O Antony! O thou Arabian bird!
*Enobarbus.* Would you praise Caesar, say 'Caesar': go no
further.
*Agrippa.* Indeed he plied them both with excellent praises.
15 *Enobarbus.* But he loves Caesar best, yet he loves Antony:
Hoo! hearts, tongues, figures, scribes, bards, poets, cannot
Think, speak, cast, write, sing, number — hoo! — *ironic*
His love to Antony. But as for Caesar,
Kneel down, kneel down, and wonder.
*Agrippa.* Both he loves.
*Enobarbus.* They are his shards, and he their beetle. [*Trumpet
20 within.*] So —
This is to horse. Adieu, noble Agrippa.
*Agrippa.* Good fortune, worthy soldier, and farewell!

---

III, ii, 1 *parted* departed 3 *sealing* concluding agreements 6 *green-sickness*
(traditionally the disease of lovesick girls: Lepidus is likened to one in his
relations to Caesar and Antony) 12 *Arabian bird* i.e. unique (like the
mythical phoenix, of which only one was supposed to exist at a time)
20 *shards* wings

*Enter Caesar, Antony, Lepidus, and Octavia.*

*Antony.*  No further, sir.

*Caesar.*  You take from me a great part of myself;
  Use me well in't. Sister, prove such a wife                    25
  As my thoughts make thee, and as my farthest
    band
  Shall pass on thy approof. Most noble Antony,
  Let not the piece of virtue which is set
  Betwixt us as the cement of our love
  To keep it builded, be the ram to batter                      30
  The fortress of it: for better might we
  Have loved without this mean, if on both parts
  This be not cherished.

*Antony.*                        Make me not offended
  In your distrust.

*Caesar.*            I have said.

*Antony.*                          You shall not find,
  Though you be therein curious, the least cause                 35
  For what you seem to fear. So the gods keep you
  And make the hearts of Romans serve your ends!
  We will here part.

*Caesar.*  Farewell, my dearest sister, fare thee well.
  The elements be kind to thee, and make                        40
  Thy spirits all of comfort: fare thee well.

*Octavia.*  My noble brother!

*Antony.*  The April's in her eyes: it is love's spring,
  And these the showers to bring it on. Be cheerful.

*Octavia.*  Sir, look well to my husband's house; and —

---

26–27 *as my farthest . . . approof* such as I will give my uttermost bond that
you will prove to be  28 *piece* paragon  32 *mean* intermediary  35 *curious*
punctiliously exacting

45 *Caesar.*                                                  What,
   Octavia?
*Octavia.*   I'll tell you in your ear.
*Antony.* Her tongue will not obey her heart, nor can
   Her heart inform her tongue — the swan's down-feather
   That stands upon the swell at full of tide,
50 And neither way inclines.
*Enobarbus.* Will Caesar weep?
*Agrippa.*                        He has a cloud in's face.
*Enobarbus.* He were the worse for that, were he a horse;
   So is he, being a man.
*Agrippa.*                        Why, Enobarbus,
   When Antony found Julius Caesar dead,
55 He cried almost to roaring; and he wept
   When at Philippi he found Brutus slain.
*Enobarbus.* That year indeed he was troubled with a rheum.
   What willingly he did confound he wailed,
   Believe't, till I wept too.
*Caesar.*                        No, sweet Octavia,
60 You shall hear from me still: the time shall not
   Outgo my thinking on you.
*Antony.*                        Come, sir, come,
   I'll wrestle with you in my strength of love:
   Look, here I have you; thus I let you go,
   And give you to the gods.
*Caesar.*                        Adieu, be happy!
65 *Lepidus.* Let all the number of the stars give light
   To thy fair way!

---

48–50 *the swan's . . . inclines* i.e. her feelings for husband and brother are
evenly balanced   51–59 (Enobarbus and Agrippa talk aside)   52 *horse*
(horses without white markings on the face were thought to be ill-tempered)
57 *rheum* running at the eyes   58 *confound* destroy   60–61 *the time . . . you*
i.e. my thoughts of you will not be left behind (as in a race) by time

*Caesar.*                Farewell, farewell!        *Kisses Octavia.*
*Antony.*                                Farewell!
                                *Trumpets sound. Exeunt.*

*Enter Cleopatra, Charmian, Iras, and Alexas.*        III, iii

*Cleopatra.* Where is the fellow?
*Alexas.*                        Half afeard to come.
*Cleopatra.* Go to, go to.

*Enter the Messenger as before.*

                        Come hither, sir.
*Alexas.*                                Good Majesty,
    Herod of Jewry dare not look upon you
    But when you are well pleased.
*Cleopatra.*                        That Herod's head
    I'll have: but how, when Antony is gone        5
    Through whom I might command it? Come thou near.
*Messenger.* Most gracious Majesty!
*Cleopatra.* Didst thou behold Octavia?
*Messenger.* Ay, dread Queen.
*Cleopatra.* Where.                                10
*Messenger.* Madam, in Rome.
    I looked her in the face, and saw her led
    Between her brother and Mark Antony.
*Cleopatra.* Is she as tall as me?
*Messenger.*                        She is not, madam.
*Cleopatra.* Didst hear her speak? Is she shrill-tongued or
    low?                                            15

III, iii, 3 *Herod* i.e. even Herod (traditionally represented as a tyrant)

*Messenger.* Madam, I heard her speak; she is low-voiced.

*Cleopatra.* That's not so good. He cannot like her long.

*Charmian.* Like her? O Isis! 'tis impossible.

*Cleopatra.* I think so, Charmian. Dull of tongue, and
dwarfish.

20     What majesty is in her gait? Remember,
If e'er thou lookedst on majesty.

*Messenger.*                   She creeps:
Her motion and her station are as one.
She shows a body rather than a life,
A statue than a breather.

*Cleopatra.*             Is this certain?

*Messenger.* Or I have no observance.

25 *Charmian.*                 Three in Egypt
Cannot make better note.

*Cleopatra.*             He's very knowing,
I do perceive't. There's nothing in her yet.
The fellow has good judgment.

*Charmian.*              Excellent.

*Cleopatra.* Guess at her years, I prithee.

*Messenger.*               Madam,
She was a widow —

30 *Cleopatra.*          Widow? Charmian, hark.

*Messenger.* And I do think she's thirty.

*Cleopatra.* Bear'st thou her face in mind? is't long or round?

*Messenger.* Round even to faultiness.

*Cleopatra.* For the most part, too, they are foolish that are
so.

35     Her hair, what color?

*Messenger.* Brown, madam; and her forehead
As low as she would wish it.

17 *good* i.e. as I am   22 *Her . . . one* even in motion she is still   32 *long or round* (thought to be signs, respectively, of prudence and folly)

*Cleopatra.*                    There's gold for thee.
  Thou must not take my former sharpness ill;
  I will employ thee back again: I find thee
  Most fit for business. Go, make thee ready;                    40
  Our letters are prepared.          *[Exit Messenger.]*
*Charmian.*                  A proper man.
*Cleopatra.* Indeed he is so: I repent me much
  That so I harried him. Why, methinks, by him,
  This creature 's no such thing.
*Charmian.*                        Nothing, madam.
*Cleopatra.* The man hath seen some majesty, and should
    know.                                                            45
*Charmian.* Hath he seen majesty? Isis else defend,
  And serving you so long!
*Cleopatra.* I have one thing more to ask him yet, good
    Charmian;
  But 'tis no matter, thou shalt bring him to me
  Where I will write. All may be well enough.
*Charmian.* I warrant you, madam.          *Exeunt.*          50

❋

*Enter Antony and Octavia.*                          III, iv

*Antony.* Nay, nay, Octavia, not only that,
  That were excusable, that and thousands more
  Of semblable import — but he hath waged
  New wars 'gainst Pompey; made his will, and read it
  To public ear;                                                    5
  Spoke scantly of me: when perforce he could not

41 *proper* attractive  43 *harried* mistreated  44 *no such thing* nothing much
III, iv, 3 *semblable* like  4 *read it* (to show the public what benefactions
they might expect from him)

But pay me terms of honor, cold and sickly
He vented them, most narrow measure lent me;
When the best hint was given him, he not took't,
Or did it from his teeth.

10 *Octavia.* O, my good lord,
Believe not all, or if you must believe,
Stomach not all. A more unhappy lady,
If this division chance, ne'er stood between,
Praying for both parts.

15 The good gods will mock me presently
When I shall pray 'O, bless my lord and husband!'
Undo that prayer by crying out as loud
'O, bless my brother!' Husband win, win brother,
Prays, and destroys the prayer; no midway
'Twixt these extremes at all.

20 *Antony.* Gentle Octavia,
Let your best love draw to that point which seeks
Best to preserve it. If I lose mine honor,
I lose myself: better I were not yours
Than yours so branchless. But, as you requested,

25 Yourself shall go between 's: the mean time, lady,
I'll raise the preparation of a war
Shall stain your brother. Make your soonest haste;
So your desires are yours.

*Octavia.* Thanks to my lord.
The Jove of power make me most weak, most weak,

30 Your reconciler! Wars 'twixt you twain would be
As if the world should cleave, and that slain men
Should solder up the rift.
*Antony.* When it appears to you where this begins,

8 *narrow measure* little credit  10 *from his teeth* grudgingly  12 *Stomach*
resent  15 *presently* at once  24 *branchless* pruned (of my honors)  27 *stain*
eclipse

Turn your displeasure that way, for our faults
Can never be so equal that your love                    35
Can equally move with them. Provide your going;
Choose your own company, and command what cost
Your heart has mind to.                    *Exeunt.*

*Enter Enobarbus and Eros.*                    III, v

*Enobarbus.* How now, friend Eros?
*Eros.* There's strange news come, sir.
*Enobarbus.* What, man?
*Eros.* Caesar and Lepidus have made wars upon Pompey.
*Enobarbus.* This is old. What is the success?                    5
*Eros.* Caesar, having made use of him in the wars 'gainst
    Pompey, presently denied him rivality, would not let
    him partake in the glory of the action; and not resting
    here, accuses him of letters he had formerly wrote to
    Pompey; upon his own appeal, seizes him; so the poor    10
    third is up till death enlarge his confine.
*Enobarbus.* Then, world, thou hast a pair of chaps, no more;
    And throw between them all the food thou hast,
    They'll grind the one the other. Where's Antony?
*Eros.* He's walking in the garden – thus, and spurns        15
    The rush that lies before him; cries 'Fool Lepidus!'
    And threats the throat of that his officer
    That murd'red Pompey.
*Enobarbus.*                    Our great navy 's rigged.
*Eros.* For Italy and Caesar. More, Domitius:
    My lord desires you presently. My news                    20
    I might have told hereafter.

III, v, 5 *success* sequel   6 *wars* (a new outbreak, in which Pompey was
defeated)   7 *rivality* partnership   10 *appeal* accusation   11 *up* jailed   12
*chaps* jaws   17 *that his officer* that officer of his

*Enobarbus.*        'Twill be naught;
 But let it be. Bring me to Antony.
*Eros.* Come, sir.         *Exeunt.*

III, vi    *Enter Agrippa, Maecenas, and Caesar.*

 *Caesar.* Contemning Rome, he has done all this and more
 In Alexandria. Here's the manner of't:
 I' th' market place on a tribunal silvered,
 Cleopatra and himself in chairs of gold
5 Were publicly enthroned; at the feet sat
 Caesarion, whom they call my father's son,
 And all the unlawful issue that their lust
 Since then hath made between them. Unto her
 He gave the stablishment of Egypt; made her
10 Of lower Syria, Cyprus, Lydia,
 Absolute queen.
 *Maecenas.*   This in the public eye?
 *Caesar.* I' th' common show-place, where they exercise.
 His sons he there proclaimed the kings of kings:
 Great Media, Parthia, and Armenia
15 He gave to Alexander; to Ptolemy he assigned
 Syria, Cilicia, and Phoenicia. She
 In th' habiliments of the goddess Isis
 That day appeared, and oft before gave audience,
 As 'tis reported, so.
 *Maecenas.*   Let Rome be thus
 Informed.

III, vi, 1 *Contemning* scorning 6 *my father's* (Octavius, though actually a
nephew, had been adopted by Julius Caesar) 9 *stablishment* rule 17 *Isis*
(cf. I, ii, 60n.)

*Agrippa.*      Who, queasy with his insolence                    20
   Already, will their good thoughts call from him.
*Caesar.* The people know it, and have now received
   His accusations.
*Agrippa.*             Who does he accuse?
*Caesar.* Caesar, and that, having in Sicily
   Sextus Pompeius spoiled, we had not rated him        25
   His part o' th' isle. Then does he say he lent me
   Some shipping unrestored. Lastly, he frets
   That Lepidus of the triumvirate
   Should be deposed; and, being, that we detain
   All his revenue.
*Agrippa.*             Sir, this should be answered.        30
*Caesar.* 'Tis done already, and the messenger gone.
   I have told him Lepidus was grown too cruel,
   That he his high authority abused
   And did deserve his change. For what I have conquered,
   I grant him part; but then in his Armenia,                35
   And other of his conquered kingdoms, I
   Demand the like.
*Maecenas.*             He'll never yield to that.
*Caesar.* Nor must not then be yielded to in this.

*Enter Octavia with her Train.*

*Octavia.* Hail, Caesar, and my lord, hail, most dear Caesar!
*Caesar.* That ever I should call thee castaway!            40
*Octavia.* You have not called me so, nor have you cause.
*Caesar.* Why have you stol'n upon us thus? You come not
   Like Caesar's sister. The wife of Antony
   Should have an army for an usher, and
   The neighs of horse to tell of her approach            45

20 *queasy* nauseated   25 *spoiled* despoiled   *rated* allotted   26 *isle* i.e. Sicily

Long ere she did appear. The trees by th' way
Should have borne men, and expectation fainted,
Longing for what it had not. Nay, the dust
Should have ascended to the roof of heaven,
Raised by your populous troops. But you are
50      come
A market-maid to Rome, and have prevented
The ostentation of our love; which, left unshown,
Is often left unloved. We should have met you
By sea and land, supplying every stage
With an augmented greeting.

55 *Octavia.*                         Good my lord,
To come thus was I not constrained, but did it
On my free will. My lord, Mark Antony,
Hearing that you prepared for war, acquainted
My grievèd ear withal; whereon I begged
His pardon for return.

60 *Caesar.*                         Which soon he granted,
Being an abstract 'tween his lust and him.
*Octavia.* Do not say so, my lord.
*Caesar.*                         I have eyes upon him,
And his affairs come to me on the wind.
Where is he now?
*Octavia.*                 My lord, in Athens.
65 *Caesar.* No, my most wrongèd sister, Cleopatra
Hath nodded him to her. He hath given his empire
Up to a whore, who now are levying
The kings o' th' earth for war. He hath assembled
Bocchus, the king of Libya; Archelaus,
70      Of Cappadocia; Philadelphos, king
Of Paphlagonia; the Thracian king, Adallas;

53 *left unloved* thought to be unfelt   61 *abstract* short-cut

King Mauchus of Arabia; King of Pont;
Herod of Jewry; Mithridates, king
Of Comagene; Polemon and Amyntas,
The kings of Mede and Lycaonia; with a                    75
More larger list of sceptres.

*Octavia.*                    Ay me most wretched,
That have my heart parted betwixt two friends
That do afflict each other!

*Caesar.*                    Welcome hither.
Your letters did withhold our breaking forth,
Till we perceived both how you were wrong led                    80
And we in negligent danger. Cheer your heart:
Be you not troubled with the time, which drives
O'er your content these strong necessities;
But let determined things to destiny
Hold unbewailed their way. Welcome to Rome,                    85
Nothing more dear to me. You are abused
Beyond the mark of thought: and the high gods,
To do you justice, makes his ministers
Of us and those that love you. Best of comfort,
And ever welcome to us.

*Agrippa.*                    Welcome, lady.                    90

*Maecenas.* Welcome, dear madam.
Each heart in Rome does love and pity you.
Only th' adulterous Antony, most large
In his abominations, turns you off
And gives his potent regiment to a trull                    95
That noises it against us.

*Octavia.*                    Is it so, sir?

72 *Mauchus* (so spelled in folio; Plutarch reads 'Malchus,' and North's
translation 'Manchus')   81 *negligent danger* danger through negligence
86 *abused* betrayed (by Antony)   87 *mark* reach   88 *makes his* make their
93 *large* uninhibited   95 *regiment* rule   *trull* harlot   96 *noises it* clamors

*Treachery from Caesar.*

*Caesar.* Most certain. Sister, welcome. Pray you
  Be ever known to patience. My dear'st sister!     *Exeunt.*

❁

III, vii            *Enter Cleopatra and Enobarbus.*

*Cleopatra.* I will be even with thee, doubt it not.
*Enobarbus.* But why, why, why?
*Cleopatra.* Thou hast forspoke my being in these wars,
  And say'st it is not fit.
*Enobarbus.*            Well, is it, is it?
*Cleopatra.* Is't not denounced against us? Why should not
5   we
  Be there in person?
*Enobarbus.*      [*aside*] Well, I could reply:
  If we should serve with horse and mares together,
  The horse were merely lost; the mares would bear
  A soldier and his horse.
*Cleopatra.*            What is't you say?
10 *Enobarbus.* Your presence needs must puzzle Antony;
  Take from his heart, take from his brain, from's time,
  What should not then be spared. He is already
  Traduced for levity; and 'tis said in Rome
  That Photinus an eunuch and your maids
  Manage this war.
15 *Cleopatra.*           Sink Rome, and their tongues rot
  That speak against us! A charge we bear i' th' war,
  And as the president of my kingdom will
  Appear there for a man. Speak not against it,
  I will not stay behind.

98 *Be . . . patience* be always calm    III, vii, 3 *forspoke* opposed    5 *denounced*
declared    8 *merely* entirely    10 *puzzle* paralyze    16 *charge* responsibility

*Enter Antony and Canidius.*

*Enobarbus.*                    Nay, I have done.
  Here comes the Emperor.
*Antony.*                           Is it not strange, Canidius,          20
  That from Tarentum and Brundusium
  He could so quickly cut the Ionian sea
  And take in Toryne? — You have heard on't, sweet?
*Cleopatra.*  Celerity is never more admired
  Than by the negligent. *sarcastic*
*Antony.*                        A good rebuke,          25
  Which might have well becomed the best of men
  To taunt at slackness. Canidius, we
  Will fight with him by sea.
*Cleopatra.*                        By sea; what else?
*Canidius.*  Why will my lord do so?
*Antony.*                           For that he dares us to't.
*Enobarbus.*  So hath my lord dared him to single fight.          30
*Canidius.*  Ay, and to wage this battle at Pharsalia,
  Where Caesar fought with Pompey. But these offers,
  Which serve not for his vantage, he shakes off;
  And so should you.
*Enobarbus.*            Your ships are not well manned;
  Your mariners are muleters, reapers, people          35
  Ingrossed by swift impress. In Caesar's fleet
  Are those that often have 'gainst Pompey fought;
  Their ships are yare; yours, heavy: no disgrace
  Shall fall you for refusing him at sea,
  Being prepared for land.
*Antony.*                        By sea, by sea.          40

23 *take in* seize  29 *For that* because  35 *muleters* mule-drivers, i.e. peasants
36 *Ingrossed* collected wholesale  *impress* draft  38 *yare* nimble  39 *you*
to you

95

Antony is challenged here.

*Enobarbus.* Most worthy sir, you therein throw **away**
    The absolute soldiership you have by land,
    Distract your army, which doth most consist
    Of war-marked footmen, leave unexecuted
45    Your own renownèd knowledge, quite forgo
    The way which promises assurance, and
    Give up yourself merely to chance and hazard
    From firm security.
*Antony.*               I'll fight at sea.
*Cleopatra.* I have sixty sails, Caesar none better.
50 *Antony.* Our overplus of shipping will we burn,
    And with the rest full-manned, from th' head of **Actium**
    Beat the approaching Caesar. But if we fail,
    We then can do't at land.

*Enter a Messenger.*

                Thy business?
*Messenger.* The news is true, my lord, he is descried;
55    Caesar has taken Toryne.
*Antony.* Can he be there in person? 'Tis impossible;
    Strange that his power should be. Canidius,
    Our nineteen legions thou shalt hold by land
    And our twelve thousand horse. We'll to our ship.
    Away, my Thetis!

*Enter a Soldier.*

60                How now, worthy soldier?
*Soldier.* O noble Emperor, do not fight by sea,
    Trust not to rotten planks. Do you misdoubt
    This sword and these my wounds? Let the Egyptians
    And the Phoenicians go a-ducking: we

43 *Distract* divide  57 *power* army  60 *Thetis* name of a sea goddess

Have used to conquer standing on the earth          65
And fighting foot to foot.

*Antony.*                        Well, well, away!
                    *Exit Antony [with] Cleopatra and Enobarbus.*

*Soldier.* By Hercules, I think I am i' th' right.

*Canidius.* Soldier, thou art; but his whole action grows
    Not in the power on't: so our leader 's led,
    And we are women's men.

*Soldier.*                        You keep by land          70
    The legions and the horse whole, do you not?

*Canidius.* Marcus Octavius, Marcus Justeius,
    Publicola, and Caelius are for sea;
    But we keep whole by land. This speed of Caesar's
    Carries beyond belief.

*Soldier.*                        While he was yet in Rome,          75
    His power went out in such distractions as
    Beguiled all spies.

*Canidius.*              Who's his lieutenant, hear you?

*Soldier.* They say, one Taurus.

*Canidius.*                        Well I know the man.

                    *Enter a Messenger.*

*Messenger.* The Emperor calls Canidius.

*Canidius.* With news the time 's with labor and throws forth 80
    Each minute some.                        *Exeunt.*

68–69 *his . . . on't* his plan of action does not spring from a right estimate
of the nature of his strength   75 *Carries* i.e. like an arrow   76 *distractions*
detachments   77 *Beguiled* deceived   80 *throws* i.e. as an animal 'throws,'
gives birth to, its young

III, viii              *Enter Caesar, with his Army, marching.*

*Caesar.* Taurus!
*Taurus.* My lord?
*Caesar.* Strike not by land; keep whole, provoke not battle
  Till we have done at sea. Do not exceed
5  The prescript of this scroll. Our fortune lies
  Upon this jump.          *Exit [with Taurus and the Army]*

III, ix              *Enter Antony and Enobarbus.*

*Antony.* Set we our squadrons on yond side o' th' hill
  In eye of Caesar's battle; from which place
  We may the number of the ships behold,
  And so proceed accordingly.     *Exit [with Enobarbus].*

III, x    *Canidius marcheth with his land army one way over the
      stage, and Taurus, the lieutenant of Caesar, the other
      way. After their going in is heard the noise of a sea-
      fight. Alarum. Enter Enobarbus.*

*Enobarbus.* Naught, naught, all naught! I can behold no
    longer.
  Th' Antoniad, the Egyptian admiral,
  With all their sixty, fly and turn the rudder:
  To see't mine eyes are blasted.

              *Enter Scarus.*

*Scarus.*                    Gods and goddesses,
  All the whole synod of them!
5 *Enobarbus.*                  What's thy passion?
*Scarus.* The greater cantle of the world is lost

---

III, viii, 6 *jump* chance   III, ix, 2 *battle* battle-line   III, x, 1 *Naught* i.e.
all's come to naught   2 *admiral* flagship   5 *synod* assembly   6 *cantle*
piece

With very ignorance; we have kissed away
Kingdoms and provinces.
*Enobarbus.*                    How appears the fight?
*Scarus.* On our side like the tokened pestilence
   Where death is sure. Yon ribaudred nag of Egypt –    10
   Whom leprosy o'ertake! – i' th' midst o' th' fight,
   When vantage like a pair of twins appeared,
   Both as the same, or rather ours the elder,
   The breese upon her, like a cow in June,
   Hoists sails, and flies.                              15
*Enobarbus.* That I beheld:
   Mine eyes did sicken at the sight, and could not
   Endure a further view.
*Scarus.*                    She once being loofed,
   The noble ruin of her magic, Antony,
   Claps on his sea-wing, and (like a doting mallard)    20
   Leaving the fight in heighth, flies after her.
   I never saw an action of such shame; *decadence*
   Experience, manhood, honor, ne'er before
   Did violate so itself.
*Enobarbus.*                    Alack, alack!

*Enter Canidius.*

*Canidius.* Our fortune on the sea is out of breath,    25
   And sinks most lamentably. Had our general
   Been what he knew himself, it had gone well.
   O, he has given example for our flight
   Most grossly by his own.

9 *like . . . pestilence* like the plague when its certain symptoms have been
seen   10 *ribaudred* foul, obscene (many editors read 'ribald-rid,' but the
meaning is the same)   13 *elder* i.e. superior   14 *breese* stinging fly (with
pun on 'breeze')   18 *loofed* luffed, turned to the wind to fly (?) disen-
gaged (?)   20 *doting mallard* lovesick wild duck   27 *what . . . himself* his
true self (as a great soldier)

99

*Enobarbus.*              Ay, are you thereabouts?
30   Why then, good night indeed.

*Canidius.* Toward Peloponnesus are they fled.

*Scarus.* 'Tis easy to't; and there I will attend
    What further comes.

*Canidius.*          To Caesar will I render
    My legions and my horse; six kings already
    Show me the way of yielding.

35 *Enobarbus.*           I'll yet follow
    The wounded chance of Antony, though my reason
    Sits in the wind against me.        *[Exeunt.]*

III, xi               *Enter Antony with Attendants.*

*Antony.* Hark! the land bids me tread no more upon't,
    It is ashamed to bear me. Friends, come hither.
    I am so lated in the world that I
    Have lost my way for ever. I have a ship
5   Laden with gold: take that, divide it. Fly,
    And make your peace with Caesar.

*Omnes.*              Fly? Not we.

*Antony.* I have fled myself, and have instructed cowards
    To run and show their shoulders. Friends, be gone.
    I have myself resolved upon a course
10   Which has no need of you. Be gone.
    My treasure 's in the harbor. Take it! O,
    I followed that I blush to look upon.
    My very hairs do mutiny: for the white
    Reprove the brown for rashness, and they them

29 *are you thereabouts* i.e. is that where your thoughts are   36 *chance* fortunes   37 *Sits . . . me* dissuades   III, xi, 3 *so . . . world* i.e. like a traveller
after nightfall   12 *that* what

For fear and doting. Friends, be gone, you shall          15
Have letters from me to some friends that will
Sweep your way for you. Pray you look not sad
Nor make replies of loathness; take the hint
Which my despair proclaims. Let that be left
Which leaves itself. To the seaside straightway!          20
I will possess you of that ship and treasure.
Leave me, I pray, a little: pray you now,
Nay, do so; for indeed I have lost command,
Therefore I pray you. I'll see you by and by.  *Sits down.*

*Enter Cleopatra led by Charmian, [Iras,] and Eros.*

*Eros.* Nay, gentle madam, to him, comfort him.          25
*Iras.* Do, most dear Queen.
*Charmian.* Do? Why, what else?
*Cleopatra.* Let me sit down. O Juno!
*Antony.* No, no, no, no, no.
*Eros.* See you here, sir?                                30
*Antony.* O fie, fie, fie!
*Charmian.* Madam!
*Iras.* Madam, O good Empress!
*Eros.* Sir, sir!
*Antony.* Yes, my lord, yes. He at Philippi kept          35
   His sword e'en like a dancer, while I struck
   The lean and wrinkled Cassius; and 'twas I
   That the mad Brutus ended: he alone
   Dealt on lieutenantry, and no practice had
   In the brave squares of war: yet now — No matter.     40
*Cleopatra.* Ah, stand by.

17 *Sweep* i.e. with Caesar  19 *that* i.e. himself  23-24 *I ... pray you* i.e. I
have lost the right to order you, so I entreat you  35-36 *kept ... dancer* i.e.
never drew his sword  39 *Dealt on lieutenantry* relied on subordinates
40 *squares* squadrons

*Eros.* The Queen, my lord, the Queen.

*Iras.* Go to him, madam, speak to him;
   He is unqualitied with very shame.

45 *Cleopatra.* Well then, sustain me. O!

*Eros.* Most noble sir, arise. The Queen approaches.
   Her head's declined, and death will seize her, but
   Your comfort makes the rescue.

*Antony.* I have offended reputation,
   A most unnoble swerving.

50 *Eros.*                              Sir, the Queen.

*Antony.* O, whither hast thou led me, Egypt? See
   How I convey my shame out of thine eyes
   By looking back what I have left behind
   'Stroyed in dishonor.

*Cleopatra.*                    O my lord, my lord,
55   Forgive my fearful sails: I little thought
   You would have followed.

*Antony.*                              Egypt, thou knew'st too well
   My heart was to thy rudder tied by th' strings,
   And thou shouldst tow me after. O'er my spirit
   Thy full supremacy thou knew'st, and that
60   Thy beck might from the bidding of the gods
   Command me.

*Cleopatra.*        O, my pardon!

*Antony.*                              Now I must
   To the young man send humble treaties, dodge
   And palter in the shifts of lowness, who
   With half the bulk o' th' world played as I pleased,
65   Making and marring fortunes. You did know

---

44 *unqualitied* unmanned  47 *but* unless  53 *By looking back* i.e. by averting
my eyes from yours and looking back at  60 *beck* beckoning  62 *treaties*
proposals  63 *palter . . . lowness* i.e. use the tricks to which a man brought
low is reduced

How much you were my conqueror, and that
My sword, made weak by my affection, would
Obey it on all cause.
*Cleopatra.*              Pardon, pardon!
*Antony.* Fall not a tear, I say: one of them rates
All that is won and lost. Give me a kiss;                    70
Even this repays me. We sent our schoolmaster.
Is 'a come back? Love, I am full of lead.
Some wine, within there, and our viands! Fortune knows
We scorn her most when most she offers blows. *Exeunt.*

*Enter Caesar, Agrippa, Dolabella, [Thidias,] with others.*   III, x

*Caesar.* Let him appear that's come from Antony.
Know you him?
*Dolabella.*              Caesar, 'tis his schoolmaster:
An argument that he is plucked, when hither
He sends so poor a pinion of his wing,
Which had superfluous kings for messengers             5
Not many moons gone by.

*Enter Ambassador from Antony.*

*Caesar.*                    Approach and speak.
*Ambassador.* Such as I am, I come from Antony.
I was of late as petty to his ends
As is the morn-dew on the myrtle leaf
To his grand sea.
*Caesar.*              Be't so. Declare thine office.        10

69 *Fall* let fall  *rates* equals  71 *schoolmaster* i.e. his children's tutor  72 *lead*
i.e. grief  III, xii, 10 *sea* i.e. the ultimate source of dew

*Ambassador.* Lord of his fortunes he salutes thee, and
    Requires to live in Egypt; which not granted,
    He lessons his requests, and to thee sues
    To let him breathe between the heavens and earth,
15  A private man in Athens: this for him.
    Next, Cleopatra does confess thy greatness,
    Submits her to thy might, and of thee craves
    The circle of the Ptolemies for her heirs,
    Now hazarded to thy grace.
*Caesar.*                     For Antony,
20  I have no ears to his request. The Queen
    Of audience nor desire shall fail, so she
    From Egypt drive her all-disgracèd friend
    Or take his life there. This if she perform,
    She shall not sue unheard. So to them both.
*Ambassador.* Fortune pursue thee!
25 *Caesar.*              Bring him through the bands.
                          *[Exit Ambassador.]*
    *[To Thidias]* To try thy eloquence now 'tis time.
      Dispatch.
    From Antony win Cleopatra: promise,
    And in our name, what she requires; add more,
    From thine invention, offers. Women are not
30  In their best fortunes strong, but want will perjure
    The ne'er-touched Vestal. Try thy cunning, Thidias;
    Make thine own edict for thy pains, which we
    Will answer as a law.
*Thidias.*             Caesar, I go.
*Caesar.* Observe how Antony becomes his flaw,

---

12 *Requires* requests  13 *lessons* disciplines  14 *breathe* i.e. go on living
18 *circle* crown  19 *hazarded . . . grace* dependent on your mercy  21 *audience* a hearing  *so* provided  25 *bands* of troops  32 *Make . . . edict* name
your own price (as reward)  34 *becomes his flaw* takes his fall

And what thou think'st his very action speaks          35
In every power that moves.
*Thidias.*                    Caesar, I shall.          *Exeunt.*

*Enter Cleopatra, Enobarbus, Charmian, and Iras.*          III, xiii

*Cleopatra.* What shall we do, Enobarbus?
*Enobarbus.*                    Think, and die.
*Cleopatra.* Is Antony or we in fault for this?
*Enobarbus.* Antony only, that would make his will
    Lord of his reason. What though you fled
    From that great face of war, whose several ranges          5
    Frighted each other? Why should he follow?
    The itch of his affection should not then
    Have nicked his captainship, at such a point,
    When half to half the world opposed, he being
    The merèd question. 'Twas a shame no less          10
    Than was his loss, to course your flying flags
    And leave his navy gazing.
*Cleopatra.*                    Prithee peace.

*Enter the Ambassador, with Antony.*

*Antony.* Is that his answer?
*Ambassador.* Ay, my lord.
*Antony.* The Queen shall then have courtesy, so she          15
    Will yield us up.
*Ambassador.*          He says so.
*Antony.*                    Let her know't.

35–36 *And . . . moves* and what you think his every move reveals  III, xiii, 3
*will* desire   5 *ranges* battle lines   8 *nicked* got the better of   10 *merèd*
*question* sole cause (?) decisive factor (?)   11 *course* chase

To the boy Caesar send this grizzled head,
And he will fill thy wishes to the brim
With principalities.

*Cleopatra.*                That head, my lord?

20  *Antony.*  To him again! Tell him he wears the rose
Of youth upon him; from which the world should **note**
Something particular. His coin, ships, legions
May be a coward's, whose ministers would prevail
Under the service of a child as soon

25  As i' th' command of Caesar. I dare him therefore
To lay his gay comparisons apart
And answer me declined, sword against sword,
Ourselves alone. I'll write it: follow me.

                    *[Exeunt Antony and Ambassador.]*

*Enobarbus.* *[aside]* Yes, like enough: high-battled Caesar will

30  Unstate his happiness and be staged to th' show
Against a sworder! I see men's judgments are
A parcel of their fortunes, and things outward
Do draw the inward quality after them
To suffer all alike. That he should dream,

35  Knowing all measures, the full Caesar will
Answer his emptiness! Caesar, thou has subdued
His judgment too.

                    *Enter a Servant.*

*Servant.*                A messenger from Caesar.
*Cleopatra.* **What**, no more ceremony? See, my women,

---

22 *Something particular* i.e. some personal heroism   26 *comparisons* i.e. all
things which give him the advantage when he compares his position with
mine   27 *declined* i.e. in years and fortune   29 *high-battled* lifted high in
strength and mood by successful armies   30 *Unstate* abdicate   30–31 *be
. . . sworder* be exposed as a public spectacle in a gladiatorial duel   32 *A
parcel* i.e. part and parcel   33 *quality* nature   34 *To . . . alike* so that both
decline together   35 *Knowing all measures* being a good judge (of men and
things)

106

Against the blown rose may they stop their nose
That kneeled unto the buds. Admit him, sir.                    40

                              *Exit Servant.*

*Enobarbus. [aside]* Mine honesty and I begin to square.
  The loyalty well held to fools does make
  Our faith mere folly: yet he that can endure
  To follow with allegiance a fall'n lord
  Does conquer him that did his master conquer          45
  And earns a place i' th' story.

                    *Enter Thidias.*

*Cleopatra.*                          Caesar's will?
*Thidias.* Hear it apart.
*Cleopatra.*                None but friends: say boldly.
*Thidias.* So, haply, are they friends to Antony.
*Enobarbus.* He needs as many, sir, as Caesar has,
  Or needs not us. If Caesar please, our master          50
  Will leap to be his friend; for us, you know,
  Whose he is we are, and that is Caesar's.
*Thidias.*                                      So.
  Thus then, thou most renowned, Caesar entreats
  Not to consider in what case thou stand'st
  Further than he is Caesar.
*Cleopatra.*                  Go on: right royal.          55
*Thidias.* He knows that you embrace not Antony
  As you did love, but as you feared him.
*Cleopatra.*                                O!
*Thidias.* The scars upon your honor therefore he
  Does pity, as constrainèd blemishes,
  Not as deserved.

---

41 *square* quarrel  48 *haply* most likely  52 *Whose . . . are* i.e. whomever
Antony belongs to, we belong to (?)  54-55 *Not . . . Caesar* i.e. not to
think about your situation beyond realizing that you have to do with (a
generous conqueror like) Caesar

60 *Cleopatra.*          He is a god, and knows
      What is most right. Mine honor was not yielded,
      But conquered merely.

   *Enobarbus.*               [*aside*] To be sure of that,
      I will ask Antony. Sir, sir, thou art so leaky
      That we must leave thee to thy sinking, for
      Thy dearest quit thee.               *Exit Enobarbus.*

65 *Thidias.*               Shall I say to Caesar
      What you require of him? For he partly begs
      To be desired to give. It much would please him
      That of his fortunes you should make a staff
      To lean upon. But it would warm his spirits

70 To hear from me you had left Antony,
      And put yourself under his shroud,
      The universal landlord.

   *Cleopatra.*               What's your name?

   *Thidias.* My name is Thidias.

   *Cleopatra.*               Most kind messenger,
      Say to great Caesar this: in deputation

75 I kiss his conqu'ring hand; tell him I am prompt
      To lay my crown at's feet, and there to kneel.
      Tell him, from his all-obeying breath, I hear
      The doom of Egypt.

   *Thidias.*               'Tis your noblest course:
      Wisdom and fortune combating together,

80 If that the former dare but what it can,
      No chance may shake it. Give me grace to lay
      My duty on your hand.

   *Cleopatra.*               Your Caesar's father oft,
      When he hath mused of taking kingdoms in,

66 *require* request   71 *shroud* shelter   74 *in deputation* i.e. through you as
deputy   77 *all-obeying* that all obey   80 *If . . . can* if discretion confines
itself to the possible   82 *My duty* i.e. a kiss

Bestowed his lips on that unworthy place,
As it rained kisses.

*Enter Antony and Enobarbus.*

*Antony.*                Favors? by Jove that thunders!          85
What art thou, fellow?
*Thidias.*                One that but performs
The bidding of the fullest man, and worthiest
To have command obeyed.
*Enobarbus.*                    [aside] You will be whipped.
*Antony.* Approach there! Ah, you kite! Now, gods and
    devils!
Authority melts from me. Of late, when I cried 'Ho!'          90
Like boys unto a muss, kings would start forth,
And cry 'Your will?' Have you no ears? I am
Antony yet.

*Enter a Servant.*

Take hence this Jack and whip him.
*Enobarbus.* [aside] 'Tis better playing with a lion's whelp
Than with an old one dying.
*Antony.*                    Moon and stars!          95
Whip him. Were't twenty of the greatest tributaries
That do acknowledge Caesar, should I find them
So saucy with the hand of she here — what's her name
Since she was Cleopatra? Whip him, fellows,
Till like a boy you see him cringe his face          100
And whine aloud for mercy. Take him hence.
*Thidias.* Mark Antony —
*Antony.*                Tug him away. Being whipped,
Bring him again. This Jack of Caesar's shall

91 *muss* scramble   93 *Jack* conceited upstart   98–99 *what's . . . Cleopatra*
(Antony implies that this common trafficker in kisses cannot be the imperial
Cleopatra)

    Bear us an errand to him. *Exeunt [Servants] with Thidias.*

105    You were half blasted ere I knew you. Ha!

    Have I my pillow left unpressed in Rome,

    Forborne the getting of a lawful race,

    And by a gem of women, to be abused

    By one that looks on feeders?

    *Cleopatra.*               Good my lord —

110  *Antony.* You have been a boggler ever:

    But when we in our viciousness grow hard

    (O misery on't!) the wise gods seel our eyes,

    In our own filth drop our clear judgments, make us

    Adore our errors, laugh at's while we strut

    To our confusion.

115  *Cleopatra.*        O, is't come to this?

    *Antony.* I found you as a morsel cold upon

    Dead Caesar's trencher: nay, you were a fragment

    Of Gneius Pompey's, besides what hotter hours,

    Unregist'red in vulgar fame, you have

120    Luxuriously picked out. For I am sure,

    Though you can guess what temperance should be,

    You know not what it is.

    *Cleopatra.*            Wherefore is this?

    *Antony.* To let a fellow that will take rewards

    And say 'God quit you!' be familiar with

125    My playfellow, your hand, this kingly seal

    And plighter of high hearts. O that I were

    Upon the hill of Basan to outroar

    The hornèd herd! for I have savage cause,

---

108 *abused* betrayed  109 *feeders* menials  110 *boggler* shifty one  112 *seel*
sew up  117 *trencher* plate  *fragment* leftover  119 *vulgar fame* common
gossip  120 *Luxuriously* lustfully  124 *quit* repay  126–28 O . . . *herd*
(Antony thinks of himself as chief among the herd of bulls of Bashan whose
roaring is described in Psalms 22:12–13—i.e. as chief cuckold among all
the lovers cuckolded by Cleopatra)

And to proclaim it civilly were like
A haltered neck which does the hangman thank     130
For being yare about him.

*Enter a Servant with Thidias.*

                         Is he whipped?
*Servant.*  Soundly, my lord.
*Antony.*                    Cried he? and begged 'a pardon?
*Servant.*  He did ask favor.
*Antony.*  If that thy father live, let him repent
Thou wast not made his daughter; and be thou sorry     135
To follow Caesar in his triumph, since
Thou hast been whipped for following him. Henceforth
The white hand of a lady fever thee,
Shake thou to look on't. Get thee back to Caesar,
Tell him thy entertainment: look thou say     140
He makes me angry with him. For he seems
Proud and disdainful, harping on what I am,
Not what he knew I was. He makes me angry,
And at this time most easy 'tis to do't,
When my good stars that were my former guides     145
Have empty left their orbs and shot their fires
Into th' abysm of hell. If he mislike
My speech and what is done, tell him he has
Hipparchus, my enfranchèd bondman, whom
He may at pleasure whip, or hang, or torture,     150
As he shall like, to quit me. Urge it thou.
Hence with thy stripes, be gone!          *Exit Thidias.*
*Cleopatra.*  Have you done yet?

---

129 *like* to act like   131 *yare* nimble   140 *entertainment* reception (here)
146 *orbs* the spheres in which they turn   149 *Hipparchus* (who had earlier
revolted to Caesar)   *enfranchèd* freed

*Antony.*                    Alack, our terrene moon
Is now eclipsed, and it portends alone
The fall of Antony.

155 *Cleopatra.*          I must stay his time.

*Antony.* To flatter Caesar, would you mingle eyes
With one that ties his points?

*Cleopatra.*              Not know me yet?

*Antony.* Cold-hearted toward me?

*Cleopatra.*              Ah, dear, if I be so,
From my cold heart let heaven engender hail,

160 And poison it in the source, and the first stone
Drop in my neck: as it determines, so
Dissolve my life! The next Caesarion smite,
Till by degrees the memory of my womb,
Together with my brave Egyptians all,

165 By the discandying of this pelleted storm,
Lie graveless, till the flies and gnats of Nile
Have buried them for prey!

*Antony.*              I am satisfied.
Caesar sits down in Alexandria, where
I will oppose his fate. Our force by land

170 Hath nobly held; our severed navy too
Have knit again, and fleet, threat'ning most sea-like.
Where hast thou been, my heart? Dost thou hear, lady?
If from the field I shall return once more
To kiss these lips, I will appear in blood;

175 I and my sword will earn our chronicle.
There's hope in't yet.

153 *our . . . moon* i.e. Cleopatra, our terrestrial Isis or moon-goddess 155
*stay his time* wait out his fury 157 *one . . . points* his valet 161 *determines*
melts 163 *the memory . . . womb* i.e. my offspring 165 *discandying* melting
(as if it were hard candy) 171 *fleet* are afloat 172 *heart* courage 174 *in
blood* (1) bloody (2) with blood up, spirited 175 *our chronicle* our place
in history

*Cleopatra.* That's my brave lord!
*Antony.* I will be treble-sinewed, hearted, breathed,
    And fight maliciously; for when mine hours
    Were nice and lucky, men did ransom lives        180
    Of me for jests; but now I'll set my teeth
    And send to darkness all that stop me. Come,
    Let's have one other gaudy night: call to me
    All my sad captains; fill our bowls once more;
    Let's mock the midnight bell.
*Cleopatra.*                          It is my birthday.        185
    I had thought t' have held it poor. But since my lord
    Is Antony again, I will be Cleopatra.
*Antony.* We will yet do well.
*Cleopatra.* Call all his noble captains to my lord.
*Antony.* Do so, we'll speak to them; and to-night I'll force   190
    The wine peep through their scars. Come on, my queen,
    There's sap in't yet! The next time I do fight,
    I'll make death love me, for I will contend
    Even with his pestilent scythe. *Exeunt [all but Enobarbus].*
*Enobarbus.* Now he'll outstare the lightning. To be furious   195
    Is to be frighted out of fear, and in that mood
    The dove will peck the estridge; and I see still
    A diminution in our captain's brain
    Restores his heart. When valor preys on reason,
    It eats the sword it fights with: I will seek        200
    Some way to leave him.                        *[Exit.]*

180 *nice* able to be 'choosy'   183 *gaudy* joyous   192 *sap* i.e. life, hope   197
*estridge* species of the hawk   201 s.D. *Exit* (folio reads 'Exeunt')

113

IV, i    *Enter Caesar, Agrippa, and Maecenas, with his Army,*
       *Caesar reading a letter.*

  *Caesar.* He calls me boy, and chides as he had power
    To beat me out of Egypt. My messenger
    He hath whipped with rods; dares me to personal combat,
    Caesar to Antony. Let the old ruffian know
5   I have many other ways to die, meantime
    Laugh at his challenge.
  *Maecenas.*              Caesar must think,
    When one so great begins to rage, he's hunted
    Even to falling. Give him no breath, but now
    Make boot of his distraction: never anger
    Made good guard for itself.
10 *Caesar.*               Let our best heads
    Know that to-morrow the last of many battles
    We mean to fight. Within our files there are,
    Of those that served Mark Antony but late,
    Enough to fetch him in. See it done,
15   And feast the army; we have store to do't,
    And they have earned the waste. Poor Antony! *Exeunt.*

IV, ii    *Enter Antony, Cleopatra, Enobarbus, Charmian, Iras,*
       *Alexas, with others.*

  *Antony.* He will not fight with me, Domitius?
  *Enobarbus.*                 No.
  *Antony.* Why should he not?
  *Enobarbus.* He thinks, being twenty times of better fortune,
    He is twenty men to one.

IV, i, 9 *boot* advantage   12 *files* troops   14 *fetch him in* capture him

*Antony.*                    To-morrow, soldier,
By sea and land I'll fight: or I will live,                    5
Or bathe my dying honor in the blood
Shall make it live again. Woo't thou fight well?
*Enobarbus.* I'll strike, and cry 'Take all!'
*Antony.*                    Well said, come on;
Call forth my household servants; let's to-night
Be bounteous at our meal.

*Enter three or four Servitors.*

                    Give me thy hand,                    10
Thou hast been rightly honest, so hast thou,
And thou, and thou, and thou: you have served me well,
And kings have been your fellows.
*Cleopatra.*                    What means this?
*Enobarbus.* 'Tis one of those odd tricks which sorrow shoots
Out of the mind.
*Antony.*                    And thou art honest too.                    15
I wish I could be made so many men,
And all of you clapped up together in
An Antony, that I might do you service
So good as you have done.
*Omnes.*                    The gods forbid!
*Antony.* Well, my good fellows, wait on me to-night:                    20
Scant not my cups, and make as much of me
As when mine empire was your fellow too
And suffered my command.
*Cleopatra.*                    What does he mean?
*Enobarbus.* To make his followers weep.
*Antony.*                    Tend me to-night;

IV, ii, 5 *or* either  8 *Take all* winner take all  13–15 (here and in ll. 23–24
Enobarbus and Cleopatra talk aside)  16 *so many men* i.e. so many men as
you are

25  May be it is the period of your duty.
    Haply you shall not see me more; or if,
    A mangled shadow. Perchance to-morrow
    You'll serve another master. I look on you
    As one that takes his leave. Mine honest friends,
30  I turn you not away, but like a master
    Married to your good service, stay till death.
    Tend me to-night two hours, I ask no more,
    And the gods yield you for't!
*Enobarbus.*                    What mean you, sir,
    To give them this discomfort? Look, they weep,
35  And I, an ass, am onion-eyed; for shame!
    Transform us not to women.
*Antony.*                    Ho, ho, ho!
    Now the witch take me if I meant it thus!
    Grace grow where those drops fall! My hearty friends,
    You take me in too dolorous a sense,
40  For I spake to you for your comfort, did desire you
    To burn this night with torches. Know, my hearts,
    I hope well of to-morrow, and will lead you
    Where rather I'll expect victorious life
    Than death and honor. Let's to supper, come,
45  And drown consideration.                    *Exeunt.*

IV, iii                *Enter a Company of Soldiers.*

    1. *Soldier.* Brother, good night: to-morrow is the day.
    2. *Soldier.* It will determine one way: fare you well.
       Heard you of nothing strange about the streets?

25 *period* end   26 *Haply* most likely   33 *yield* repay   38 *Grace grow* may
virtues spring up (with a pun on 'grace' as one name for the herb rue)

1. *Soldier.* Nothing. What news?
2. *Soldier.* Belike 'tis but a rumor. Good night to you. 5
1. *Soldier.* Well, sir, good night.

*They meet other Soldiers.*

2. *Soldier.* Soldiers, have careful watch.
3. *Soldier.* And you. Good night, good night.

*They place themselves in every corner of the stage.*

4. *Soldier.* Here we; and if to-morrow
Our navy thrive, I have an absolute hope
Our landmen will stand up.
3. *Soldier.* 'Tis a brave army, 10
And full of purpose.

*Music of the hautboys is under the stage.*

2. *Soldier.* Peace! What noise?
1. *Soldier.* List, list!
2. *Soldier.* Hark!
1. *Soldier.* Music i' th' air.
3. *Soldier.* Under the earth.
4. *Soldier.* It signs well, does it not?
3. *Soldier.* No.
1. *Soldier.* Peace, I say!
What should this mean?
2. *Soldier.* 'Tis the god Hercules, whom Antony loved, 15
Now leaves him.
1. *Soldier.* Walk; let's see if other watchmen
Do hear what we do.
2. *Soldier.* How now, masters?
*Omnes.* *(speak together)* How now?
How now? Do you hear this?

IV, iii, 8 *Here we* i.e. here is our post 13 *signs* signifies 15 *Hercules* (cf. I,
iii, 84–85n.)

*1. Soldier.*                                    Ay. Is't not strange?

*3. Soldier.* Do you hear, masters? do you hear?

20 *1. Soldier.* Follow the noise so far as we have quarter.
Let's see how it will give off.

*Omnes.* Content. 'Tis strange.                              *Exeunt.*

IV, iv              *Enter Antony and Cleopatra, with others.*

*Antony.* Eros! mine armor, Eros!

*Cleopatra.*                              Sleep a little.

*Antony.* No, my chuck. Eros, come; mine armor, Eros.

*Enter Eros [with armor].*

Come, good fellow, put thine iron on.
If fortune be not ours to-day, it is
Because we brave her. Come.

5 *Cleopatra.*                              Nay, I'll help too.
What's this for?

*Antony.*              Ah, let be, let be! Thou art
The armorer of my heart. False, false; this, this.

*Cleopatra.* Sooth, la, I'll help: thus it must be.

*Antony.*                                    Well, well,
We shall thrive now. Seest thou, my good fellow?
Go, put on thy defenses.

10 *Eros.*                              Briefly, sir.

*Cleopatra.* Is not this buckled well?

*Antony.*                              Rarely, rarely:
He that unbuckles this, till we do please
To daff't for our repose, shall hear a storm.

---

20 *as . . . quarter* as our watch extends   IV, iv, 3 *thine iron* i.e. this armor
of mine   7 *False* wrong   10 *Briefly* in a moment   13 *daff't* take it off

Thou fumblest, Eros, and my queen 's a squire
More tight at this than thou. Dispatch. O love,                    15
That thou couldst see my wars to-day, and knew'st
The royal occupation: thou shouldst see
A workman in't.

*Enter an armed Soldier.*

                    Good morrow to thee, welcome,
Thou look'st like him that knows a warlike charge.
To business that we love we rise betime                           20
And go to't with delight.
*Soldier.*                    A thousand, sir,
Early though't be, have on their riveted trim,
And at the port expect you.

*Shout. Trumpets flourish. Enter Captains and Soldiers.*

*Captain.* The morn is fair. Good morrow, General.
*All.* Good morrow, General.
*Antony.*                    'Tis well blown, lads.               25
This morning, like the spirit of a youth
That means to be of note, begins betimes.
So, so. Come, give me that: this way. Well said.
Fare thee well, dame; whate'er becomes of me,
This is a soldier's kiss. Rebukable                               30
And worthy shameful check it were to stand
On more mechanic compliment. I'll leave thee
Now like a man of steel. You that will fight,
Follow me close; I'll bring you to't. Adieu.
                    *Exeunt [Antony, Eros, Captains, and Soldiers].*

---

15 *tight* deft  18 *workman* craftsman, expert  19 *charge* duty  20 *betime*
early  22 *riveted trim* armor  23 *port* gate  25 *blown* opened (i.e. the
morning)  28 *said* done (spoken to Cleopatra, who is arming him)  31
*check* reproof  31–32 *stand . . . compliment* use more elaborate ceremony

*Charmian.* Please you retire to your chamber?

35 *Cleopatra.*                                               Lead me.
     He goes forth gallantly. That he and Caesar might
     Determine this great war in single fight!
     Then Antony — but now — Well, on.              *Exeunt.*

IV, v      *Trumpets sound. Enter Antony and Eros, [a Soldier*
           *meeting them].*

*Soldier.* The gods make this a happy day to Antony!
*Antony.* Would thou and those thy scars had once
          prevailed
     To make me fight at land!
*Soldier.*                        Hadst thou done so,
     The kings that have revolted and the soldier
5    That has this morning left thee would have still
     Followèd thy heels.
*Antony.*              Who's gone this morning?
*Soldier.*                                        Who?
     One ever near thee: call for Enobarbus,
     He shall not hear thee, or from Caesar's camp
     Say 'I am none of thine.'
*Antony.*                    What sayest thou?
*Soldier.*                                        Sir,
     He is with Caesar.
10 *Eros.*              Sir, his chests and treasure
     He has not with him.
*Antony.*              Is he gone?
*Soldier.*                        Most certain.
*Antony.* Go, Eros, send his treasure after; do it;
     Detain no jot, I charge thee. Write to him

(I will subscribe) gentle adieus and greetings;
Say that I wish he never find more cause                    15
To change a master. O, my fortunes have
Corrupted honest men! Dispatch. Enobarbus!

*Exit [with Eros and Soldier].*

*Flourish. Enter Agrippa, Caesar, with Enobarbus, and*    IV, vi
*Dolabella.*

*Caesar.* Go forth, Agrippa, and begin the fight.
Our will is Antony be took alive:
Make it so known.
*Agrippa.* Caesar, I shall.                    *[Exit.]*
*Caesar.* The time of universal peace is near.                    5
Prove this a prosp'rous day, the three-nooked world
Shall bear the olive freely.

*Enter a Messenger.*

*Messenger.*                    Antony
Is come into the field.
*Caesar.*                    Go charge Agrippa
Plant those that have revolted in the vant,
That Antony may seem to spend his fury                    10
Upon himself.                    *Exeunt [all but Enobarbus].*
*Enobarbus.* Alexas did revolt and went to Jewry on
Affairs of Antony; there did dissuade
Great Herod to incline himself to Caesar
And leave his master Antony. For this pains                    15

IV, v, 14 *subscribe* sign    IV, vi, 6 *three-nooked* three-cornered (Africa,
Asia, Europe)  9 *vant* front lines  11 *himself* i.e. his own former soldiers
13 *dissuade* i.e. from Antony

Caesar hath hanged him. Canidius and the rest
That fell away have entertainment, but
No honorable trust. I have done ill,
Of which I do accuse myself so sorely
That I will joy no more.

*Enter a Soldier of Caesar's.*

20 *Soldier.*                  Enobarbus, Antony
  Hath after thee sent all thy treasure, with
  His bounty overplus. The messenger
  Came on my guard, and at thy tent is now
  Unloading of his mules.
  *Enobarbus.*              I give it you.
25 *Soldier.* Mock not, Enobarbus.
  I tell you true. Best you safed the bringer
  Out of the host; I must attend mine office
  Or would have done't myself. Your emperor
  Continues still a Jove.                  *Exit.*
30 *Enobarbus.* I am alone the villain of the earth,
  And feel I am so most. O Antony,
  Thou mine of bounty, how wouldst thou have paid
  My better service, when my turpitude
  Thou dost so crown with gold! This blows my heart.
35   If swift thought break it not, a swifter mean
  Shall outstrike thought; but thought will do't, I feel.
  I fight against thee? No, I will go seek
  Some ditch wherein to die: the foul'st best fits
  My latter part of life.                  *Exit.*

17 *entertainment* employment    26 *safed* gave safe conduct to    34 *blows*
makes swell    35 *thought* grief

*Alarum. Drums and Trumpets. Enter Agrippa [and*    IV, vii
*Soldiers].*

*Agrippa.* Retire. We have engaged ourselves too far.
Caesar himself has work, and our oppression
Exceeds what we expected.    *Exit [with Soldiers].*

*Alarums. Enter Antony, and Scarus wounded.*

*Scarus.* O my brave Emperor, this is fought indeed!
Had we done so at first, we had droven them home    5
With clouts about their heads.
*Antony.*    Thou bleed'st apace.
*Scarus.* I had a wound here that was like a T,
But now 'tis made an H.    *[Sound retreat] far off.*
*Antony.*    They do retire.
*Scarus.* We'll beat 'em into bench-holes. I have yet
Room for six scotches more.    10

        *Enter Eros.*

*Eros.* They are beaten, sir, and our advantage serves
For a fair victory.
*Scarus.*    Let us score their backs
And snatch 'em up, as we take hares, behind:
'Tis sport to maul a runner.
*Antony.*    I will reward thee
Once for thy sprightly comfort, and tenfold    15
For thy good valor. Come thee on.
*Scarus.*    I'll halt after. *Exeunt.*

❁

IV, vii, 1 *engaged* entangled (with the enemy)  2 *our oppression* the pressure
on us  6 *clouts* bandages  8 *H* (pun on 'ache,' which was pronounced
'aitch')  9 *bench-holes* privy holes  10 *scotches* gashes  12 *score* mark  16 *halt*
limp

**IV, viii**    *Alarum. Enter Antony again in a march; Scarus, with others.*

*Antony.* We have beat him to his camp. Run one before
     And let the Queen know of our gests. To-morrow,
     Before the sun shall see's, we'll spill the blood
     That has to-day escaped. I thank you all,
5    For doughty-handed are you, and have fought
     Not as you served the cause, but as't had been
     Each man's like mine: you have shown all Hectors.
     Enter the city, clip your wives, your friends,
     Tell them your feats, whilst they with joyful tears
10    Wash the congealment from your wounds, and kiss
     The honored gashes whole.

*Enter Cleopatra.*

               *[To Scarus]* Give me thy hand;
     To this great fairy I'll commend thy acts,
     Make her thanks bless thee. — O thou day o' th' world,
     Chain mine armed neck; leap thou, attire and all,
15    Through proof of harness to my heart, and there
     Ride on the pants triumphing.
*Cleopatra.*              Lord of lords!
     O infinite virtue, com'st thou smiling from
     The world's great snare uncaught?
*Antony.*                 My nightingale,
     We have beat them to their beds. What, girl! though gray
     Do something mingle with our younger brown, yet ha'
20    we

---

IV, viii, 2 *gests* deeds   7 *shown* proved   8 *clip* hug   12 *fairy* enchantress
15 *proof of harness* i.e. impenetrable armor   16 *Ride . . . pants* i.e. as if his
heart were a panting steed   17 *virtue* valor   18 *snare* i.e. death in war

A brain that nourishes our nerves, and can
Get goal for goal of youth. Behold this man:
Commend unto his lips thy favoring hand. —
Kiss it, my warrior. — He hath fought to-day
As if a god in hate of mankind had                          25
Destroyed in such a shape.
*Cleopatra.*                     I'll give thee, friend,
An armor all of gold; it was a king's.
*Antony.* He has deserved it, were it carbuncled
Like holy Phoebus' car. Give me thy hand.
Through Alexandria make a jolly march;                       30
Bear our hacked targets like the men that owe them.
Had our great palace the capacity
To camp this host, we all would sup together
And drink carouses to the next day's fate,
Which promises royal peril. Trumpeters,                      35
With brazen din blast you the city's ear,
Make mingle with our rattling tabourines,
That heaven and earth may strike their sounds together,
Applauding our approach.                        *Exeunt.*

*Enter a Sentry and his Company. Enobarbus follows.*     IV, ix

*Sentry.* If we be not relieved within this hour,
We must return to th' court of guard. The night
Is shiny, and they say we shall embattle
By th' second hour i' th' morn.
*1. Watchman.*                     This last day was
A shrewd one to 's.

22 *Get . . . of* hold our own with  28 *carbuncled* jewelled  29 *holy Phoebus'
car* the sun-god's chariot  31 *targets* shields  *owe* own  IV, ix, 5 *shrewd*
wicked

5 *Enobarbus.*                    O, bear me witness, night —
*2. Watchman.* What man is this?
*1. Watchman.*                    Stand close, and list him.
*Enobarbus.* Be witness to me, O thou blessèd moon,
   When men revolted shall upon record
   Bear hateful memory, poor Enobarbus did
   Before thy face repent!
*Sentry.*                    Enobarbus?
10 *2. Watchman.*                    Peace:
   Hark further.
*Enobarbus.* O sovereign mistress of true melancholy,
   The poisonous damp of night disponge upon me,
   That life, a very rebel to my will,
15   May hang no longer on me. Throw my heart
   Against the flint and hardness of my fault,
   Which, being dried with grief, will break to powder,
   And finish all foul thoughts. O Antony,
   Nobler than my revolt is infamous,
20   Forgive me in thine own particular,
   But let the world rank me in register
   A master leaver and a fugitive.
   O Antony! O Antony!                    *[Dies.]*
*1. Watchman.*                    Let's speak
   To him.
*Sentry.*   Let's hear him, for the things he speaks
   May concern Caesar.
25 *2. Watchman.*                    Let's do so. But he sleeps.
*Sentry.* Swoonds rather, for so bad a prayer as his
   Was never yet for sleep.

8-9 *When . . . memory* when traitors go down in history shamed   12 *mistress* i.e. the moon   13 *disponge* squeeze (as from a sponge)   17 *Which* (refers to *heart*)   *dried* (sorrow was thought to dry up the blood)   20 *in . . . particular* i.e. yourself   21 *in register* in its records   22 *master leaver* (1) runaway servant (2) outstanding traitor   26 *Swoonds* faints   27 *for sleep* conducive to sleep

126

*1. Watchman.*                    Go we to him.
*2. Watchman.*  Awake, sir, awake, speak to us.
*1. Watchman.*                              Hear you, sir?
*Sentry.*  The hand of death hath raught him.
                                        *Drums afar off.*
                                        Hark! The drums
Demurely wake the sleepers. Let us bear him          30
To th' court of guard: he is of note. Our hour
Is fully out.
*2. Watchman.*  Come on then,
He may recover yet.              *Exeunt [with the body].*

*Enter Antony and Scarus, with their Army.*          IV, x

*Antony.*  Their preparation is to-day by sea;
We please them not by land.
*Scarus.*                        For both, my lord.
*Antony.*  I would they'ld fight i' th' fire or i' th' air;
We'ld fight there too. But this it is, our foot
Upon the hills adjoining to the city          5
Shall stay with us — Order for sea is given;
They have put forth the haven —
Where their appointment we may best discover
And look on their endeavor.              *Exeunt.*

*Enter Caesar and his Army.*          IV, xi

*Caesar.*  But being charged, we will be still by land,
Which, as I take't, we shall; for his best force

29 *raught* reached  30 *Demurely* softly  IV, x, 4 *foot* infantry  8 *appointment* arrangement  IV, xi, 1 *But being* unless we are

Is forth to man his galleys. To the vales,
And hold our best advantage.                    *Exeunt.*

IV, xii                    *Enter Antony and Scarus.*

*Antony.* Yet they are not joined. Where yond pine does
    stand
    I shall discover all. I'll bring thee word
    Straight how 'tis like to go.                    *Exit.*
*Scarus.*                              Swallows have built
    In Cleopatra's sails their nests. The augurers
5   Say they know not, they cannot tell, look grimly,
    And dare not speak their knowledge. Antony
    Is valiant, and dejected, and by starts
    His fretted fortunes give him hope and fear
    Of what he has, and has not.
             *Alarum afar off, as at a sea-fight.*

               *Enter Antony.*

*Antony.*                              All is lost!
10  This foul Egyptian hath betrayed me:
    My fleet hath yielded to the foe, and yonder
    They cast their caps up and carouse together
    Like friends long lost. Triple-turned whore! 'tis thou
    Hast sold me to this novice, and my heart
15  Makes only wars on thee. Bid them all fly;
    For when I am revenged upon my charm,
    I have done all. Bid them all fly, be gone. *[Exit Scarus.]*
    O sun, thy uprise shall I see no more.
    Fortune and Antony part here, even here
20  Do we shake hands. All come to this? The hearts
    That spanieled me at heels, to whom I gave

IV, xii, 8 *fretted* shifting   13 *Triple-turned* i.e. from Pompey, from Julius
Caesar, and now from himself   16 *charm* enchantress

Their wishes, do discandy, melt their sweets
On blossoming Caesar; and this pine is barked,
That overtopped them all. Betrayed I am.
O this false soul of Egypt! this grave charm, 25
Whose eye becked forth my wars, and called them home,
Whose bosom was my crownet, my chief end,
Like a right gypsy hath at fast and loose
Beguiled me to the very heart of loss.
What, Eros, Eros!

*Enter Cleopatra.*

                  Ah, thou spell! Avaunt! 30
*Cleopatra.* Why is my lord enraged against his love?
*Antony.* Vanish, or I shall give thee thy deserving
And blemish Caesar's triumph. Let him take thee
And hoist thee up to the shouting plebeians;
Follow his chariot, like the greatest spot 35
Of all thy sex. Most monster-like be shown
For poor'st diminitives, for dolts, and let
Patient Octavia plough thy visage up
With her preparèd nails.       *Exit Cleopatra.*
           'Tis well th' art gone,
If it be well to live; but better 'twere 40
Thou fell'st into my fury, for one death
Might have prevented many. Eros, ho!
The shirt of Nessus is upon me; teach me,

22 *discandy* melt   23 *barked* stripped   25 *grave* deadly   27 *my crownet . . . end* the crown and purpose of my life   28 *right* true   *fast and loose* (a game) 30 *Avaunt* be gone   33 *triumph* triumphal procession (in Rome)   37 *diminitives* little people, i.e. the populace   43 *Nessus* (Fatally wounded by Hercules with a poisoned arrow, the centaur Nessus persuaded Hercules' wife to give his blood-stained shirt to her husband, telling her it would assure his love for her. The shirt so poisoned Hercules that in his agony he threw his page Lichas, who had brought it, to the skies and set about destroying himself.)

     Alcides, thou mine ancestor, thy rage.
45   Let me lodge Lichas on the horns o' th' moon
     And with those hands that grasped the heaviest club
     Subdue my worthiest self. The witch shall die.
     To the young Roman boy she hath sold me, and I fall
     Under this plot: she dies for't. Eros, ho!    *Exit.*

IV, xiii        *Enter Cleopatra, Charmian, Iras, Mardian.*

*Cleopatra.* Help me, my women: O, he's more mad
     Than Telamon for his shield; the boar of Thessaly
     Was never so embossed.
*Charmian.*            To th' monument!
     There lock yourself, and send him word you are dead.
5   The soul and body rive not more in parting
     Than greatness going off.
*Cleopatra.*           To th' monument!
     Mardian, go tell him I have slain myself:
     Say that the last I spoke was 'Antony'
     And word it, prithee, piteously. Hence, Mardian,
10  And bring me how he takes my death. To th' monument!
                                *Exeunt.*

44 *Alcides* Hercules  IV, xiii, 2 *Telamon* Ajax Telamon, who went mad
when Achilles' shield was not given to him but to his rival, Ulysses  *boar
of Thessaly* (sent by Artemis to ravage Thessaly in punishment for omitted
sacrifices)  3 *embossed* infuriated  *monument* tomb (which like other Egyptian rulers Cleopatra had prepared in advance)  5 *rive* rend

*Enter Antony and Eros.*

*Antony.* Eros, thou yet behold'st me?
*Eros.* Ay, noble lord.
*Antony.* Sometime we see a cloud that's dragonish;
  A vapor sometime like a bear or lion,
  A towered citadel, a pendant rock,
  A forkèd mountain, or blue promontory 5
  With trees upon't that nod unto the world
  And mock our eyes with air. Thou hast seen these
    signs;
  They are black Vesper's pageants.
*Eros.* Ay, my lord.
*Antony.* That which is now a horse, even with a thought
  The rack dislimns, and makes it indistinct 10
  As water is in water.
*Eros.* It does, my lord.
*Antony.* My good knave Eros, now thy captain is
  Even such a body: here I am Antony,
  Yet cannot hold this visible shape, my knave.
  I made these wars for Egypt, and the Queen, 15
  Whose heart I thought I had, for she had mine,
  Which, whilst it was mine, had annexed unto't
  A million moe, now lost — she, Eros, has
  Packed cards with Caesar, and false-played my glory
  Unto an enemy's triumph. 20
  Nay, weep not, gentle Eros, there is left us
  Ourselves to end ourselves.

IV, xiv, 8 *black Vesper's pageants* i.e. shows heralding the coming of night (as pageants used to herald the coming of a king or queen) 10 *rack* cloud *dislimns* unshapes 15 *Egypt* i.e. Cleopatra 18 *moe* more 19 *Packed* i.e. stacked the deck *false-played* falsely played away 20 *triumph* (1) victory (2) trump

*Enter Mardian.*

                                    O, thy vile lady!
She has robbed me of my sword.
*Mardian.*                              No, Antony.
My mistress loved thee and her fortunes mingled
With thine entirely.
25 *Antony.*                 Hence, saucy eunuch, peace!
She hath betrayed me and shall die the death.
*Mardian.* Death of one person can be paid but once,
And that she has discharged. What thou wouldst do
Is done unto thy hand. The last she spake
30 Was 'Antony! most noble Antony!'
Then in the midst a tearing groan did break
The name of Antony; it was divided
Between her heart and lips: she rend'red life,
Thy name so buried in her.
*Antony.*                         Dead, then?
*Mardian.*                                   Dead.
35 *Antony.* Unarm, Eros. The long day's task is done,
And we must sleep. *[to Mardian]* That thou depart'st
    hence safe
Does pay thy labor richly: go.          *Exit Mardian.*
                            Off, pluck off:
The sevenfold shield of Ajax cannot keep
The battery from my heart. O, cleave, my sides!
40 Heart, once be stronger than thy continent,
Crack thy frail case! Apace, Eros, apace.
No more a soldier. Bruisèd pieces, go;
You have been nobly borne. — From me awhile.
                                    *Exit Eros.*

23 *sword* manhood and soldiership   38 *sevenfold* having seven thicknesses
39 *battery* the battering (of grief)   40 *continent* i.e. that which contains thee

132

I will o'ertake thee, Cleopatra, and
Weep for my pardon. So it must be, for now                    45
All length is torture: since the torch is out,
Lie down, and stray no farther. Now all labor
Mars what it does; yea, very force entangles
Itself with strength: seal then, and all is done.
Eros! — I come, my queen. — Eros! — Stay for me.
Where souls do couch on flowers, we'll hand in hand,
And with our sprightly port make the ghosts gaze:
Dido and her Aeneas shall want troops,
And all the haunt be ours. — Come, Eros, Eros!

*Enter Eros.*

*Eros.*  What would my lord?
*Antony.*                            Since Cleopatra died                    55
I have lived in such dishonor that the gods
Detest my baseness. I, that with my sword
Quartered the world and o'er green Neptune's back
With ships made cities, condemn myself to lack
The courage of a woman — less noble mind                    60
Than she which by her death our Caesar tells
'I am conqueror of myself.' Thou art sworn, Eros,
That, when the exigent should come, which now
Is come indeed, when I should see behind me
Th' inevitable prosecution of                    65
Disgrace and horror, that on my command

46 *length* i.e. of life  47–49 *labor . . . strength* i.e. force is defeated by its own strength, labor by its own effort  49 *seal* bring all to a close (as in sealing a document or will)  51 *Where . . . flowers* i.e. in the Elysian fields  52 *port* behavior  53 *want troops* lack admirers (i.e. in comparison with us as faithful lovers—since Aeneas deserted Dido for Roman greatness whereas Antony is deserting Roman greatness for Cleopatra)  59 *to lack* for lacking  63 *exigent* need  65 *prosecution* pursuit

Thou then wouldst kill me. Do't, the time is come.
Thou strik'st not me, 'tis Caesar thou defeat'st.
Put color in thy cheek.

*Eros.*                    The gods withhold me!
70 Shall I do that which all the Parthian darts,
Though enemy, lost aim and could not?

*Antony.*                              Eros,
Wouldst thou be windowed in great Rome and see
Thy master thus with pleached arms, bending down
His corrigible neck, his face subdued
75 To penetrative shame, whilst the wheeled seat
Of fortunate Caesar, drawn before him, branded
His baseness that ensued?

*Eros.*                    I would not see't.

*Antony.* Come then: for with a wound I must be cured.
Draw that thy honest sword, which thou hast worn
Most useful for thy country.

80 *Eros.*                    O sir, pardon me.

*Antony.* When I did make thee free, swor'st thou not then
To do this when I bade thee? Do it at once,
Or thy precedent services are all
But accidents unpurposed. Draw, and come.

85 *Eros.* Turn from me then that noble countenance
Wherein the worship of the whole world lies.

*Antony.* Lo thee!                    [*Turns from him.*]

*Eros.* My sword is drawn.

*Antony.*                    Then let it do at once
The thing why thou hast drawn it.

*Eros.*                    My dear master,

---

72 *windowed* i.e. watching from a window  73 *pleached* folded  74 *corrigible*
submissive  75 *penetrative* penetrating  77 *His . . . ensued* the baseness of
him that followed  83 *precedent* former

134

My captain, and my emperor, let me say,                    90
　Before I strike this bloody stroke, farewell.
*Antony.* 'Tis said, man, and farewell.
*Eros.* Farewell, great chief. Shall I strike now?
*Antony.*                              Now, Eros.
*Eros.* Why, there then! Thus I do escape the sorrow
　Of Antony's death.                    *Kills himself.*
*Antony.*              Thrice-nobler than myself!        95
　Thou teachest me, O valiant Eros, what
　I should, and thou couldst not. My queen and Eros
　Have by their brave instruction got upon me
　A nobleness in record. But I will be
　A bridegroom in my death, and run into't            100
　As to a lover's bed. Come then; and, Eros,
　Thy master dies thy scholar. To do thus
　　　　　　　　　*[Falls on his sword.]*
　I learned of thee. How? not dead? not dead?
　The guard, ho! O, dispatch me!

　　　*Enter [Decretas and] a [Company of the] Guard.*

*1. Guardsman.*                    What's the noise?
*Antony.* I have done my work ill, friends. O, make an end  105
　Of what I have begun.
*2. Guardsman.*            The star is fall'n.
*1. Guardsman.* And time is at his period.
*All.*                          Alas, and woe!
*Antony.* Let him that loves me strike me dead.
*1. Guardsman.*                        Not I.

---

98–99 *got . . . record* beaten me to a noble name in history  104 S.D. *Decretas*
(the usual folio spelling of a name which also appears in the folio as *Dercetus*
and is sometimes revised by editors to *Dercetas*)  107 *period* end

*2. Guardsman.*  Nor I.

110  *3. Guardsman.*  Nor any one.        *Exeunt [the Guardsmen].*

*Decretas.*  Thy death and fortunes bid thy followers fly.
      This sword but shown to Caesar, with this tidings,
      Shall enter me with him.

*Enter Diomedes.*

*Diomedes.*  Where's Antony?

*Decretas.*                    There, Diomed, there.

*Diomedes.*                                  Lives he?

115  Wilt thou not answer, man?        *[Exit Decretas.]*

*Antony.*  Art thou there, Diomed? Draw thy sword, and
      give me
      Sufficing strokes for death.

*Diomedes.*                    Most absolute lord,
      My mistress Cleopatra sent me to thee.

*Antony.*  When did she send thee?

*Diomedes.*                              Now, my lord.

*Antony.*                                  Where is she?

*Diomedes.*  Locked in her monument. She had a prophesying
120      fear
      Of what hath come to pass; for when she saw
      (Which never shall be found) you did suspect
      She had disposed with Caesar, and that your rage
      Would not be purged, she sent you word she was dead;
125  But, fearing since how it might work, hath sent
      Me to proclaim the truth, and I am come,
      I dread, too late.

*Antony.*  Too late, good Diomed. Call my guard, I prithee.

*Diomedes.*  What ho! the Emperor's guard! the guard, what
      ho!
130  Come, your lord calls!

113 *enter* recommend   123 *disposed* made terms   124 *purged* expelled

*Enter four or five of the Guard of Antony.*

*Antony.*  Bear me, good friends, where Cleopatra bides;
'Tis the last service that I shall command you.

*1. Guardsman.*  Woe, woe are we, sir, you may not live to
    wear
All your true followers out.

*All.*                          Most heavy day!

*Antony.*  Nay, good my fellows, do not please sharp fate      135
To grace it with your sorrows. Bid that welcome
Which comes to punish us, and we punish it,
Seeming to bear it lightly. Take me up:
I have led you oft; carry me now, good friends,
And have my thanks for all.                                   140

                    *Exit [the Guard,] bearing Antony.*

*Enter Cleopatra and her Maids aloft, with Charmian and*      IV, xv
    *Iras.*

*Cleopatra.*  O Charmian, I will never go from hence.
*Charmian.*  Be comforted, dear madam.
*Cleopatra.*                          No, I will not.
All strange and terrible events are welcome,
But comforts we despise. Our size of sorrow,
Proportioned to our cause, must be as great                   5
As that which makes it.

                    *Enter Diomed [below].*

                          How now? Is he dead?
*Diomedes.*  His death's upon him, but not dead.
Look out o' th' other side your monument;
His guard have brought him thither.

                          137

*Enter, [below,] Antony, and the Guard [bearing him].*

*Cleopatra.*                                    O sun,

10    Burn the great sphere thou mov'st in, darkling stand
The varying shore o' th' world! O Antony,
Antony, Antony! Help, Charmian, help, Iras, help:
Help, friends below, let's draw him hither.

*Antony.*                                           Peace!
Not Caesar's valor hath o'erthrown Antony,

15    But Antony's hath triumphed on itself.

*Cleopatra.* So it should be, that none but Antony
Should conquer Antony, but woe 'tis so!

*Antony.* I am dying, Egypt, dying; only
I here importune death awhile, until

20    Of many thousand kisses the poor last
I lay upon thy lips.

*Cleopatra.*              I dare not, dear;
Dear my lord, pardon: I dare not,
Lest I be taken. Not th' imperious show
Of the full-fortuned Caesar ever shall

25    Be brooched with me, if knife, drugs, serpents **have**
Edge, sting, or operation. I am safe:
Your wife Octavia, with her modest eyes
And still conclusion, shall acquire no honor
Demuring upon me. But come, come, Antony!

30    Help me, my women, we must draw thee up:
Assist, good friends.

*Antony.*              O, quick, or I am gone.

*Cleopatra.* Here's sport indeed! How heavy weighs **my**
lord!

---

IV, xv, 10 *darkling* darkened  **19** *importune* beg to delay  **21** *dare not* i.e.
dare not descend to Antony's side  **25** *brooched* adorned  **28** *still conclusion*
wordless censure  **29** *Demuring* looking demurely

Our strength is all gone into heaviness:
That makes the weight. Had I great Juno's power,
The strong-winged Mercury should fetch thee up                    35
And set thee by Jove's side. Yet come a little,
Wishers were ever fools. O, come, come, come.
                    *They heave Antony aloft to Cleopatra.*
And welcome, welcome! Die when thou hast lived,
Quicken with kissing. Had my lips that power,
Thus would I wear them out.
*All.*                                        A heavy sight!                    40
*Antony.* I am dying, Egypt, dying.
    Give me some wine, and let me speak a little.
*Cleopatra.* No, let me speak, and let me rail so high
    That the false huswife Fortune break her wheel,
    Provoked by my offense.
*Antony.*                                One word, sweet queen.                    45
    Of Caesar seek your honor, with your safety. O!
*Cleopatra.* They do not go together.
*Antony.*                                        Gentle, hear me:
    None about Caesar trust but Proculeius.
*Cleopatra.* My resolution and my hands I'll trust,
    None about Caesar.                    50
*Antony.* The miserable change now at my end
    Lament nor sorrow at; but please your thoughts
    In feeding them with those my former fortunes,
    Wherein I lived the greatest prince o' th' world,
    The noblest: and do now not basely die,                    55
    Not cowardly put off my helmet to
    My countryman. A Roman, by a Roman
    Valiantly vanquished. Now my spirit is going,
    I can no more.

33 *heaviness* (with pun on 'grief')   39 *Quicken* come back to life   44 *huswife* jilt

139

*Cleopatra.*          Noblest of men, woo't die?
60    Hast thou no care of me? Shall I abide
      In this dull world, which in thy absence is
      No better than a sty? O, see, my women, *[Antony dies.]*
      The crown o' th' earth doth melt. My lord!
      O, withered is the garland of the war,
65    The soldier's pole is fall'n: young boys and girls
      Are level now with men. The odds is gone,
      And there is nothing left remarkable
      Beneath the visiting moon.          *[Swoons.]*
*Charmian.*          O, quietness, lady!
*Iras.* She's dead too, our sovereign.
*Charmian.*          Lady!
*Iras.*          Madam!
*Charmian.* O madam, madam, madam!
70 *Iras.*          Royal Egypt!
      Empress!
*Charmian.* Peace, peace, Iras!
*Cleopatra.* No more but e'en a woman, and commanded
      By such poor passion as the maid that milks
75    And does the meanest chares. It were for me
      To throw my sceptre at the injurious gods,
      To tell them that this world did equal theirs
      Till they had stol'n our jewel. All's but naught.
      Patience is sottish, and impatience does
80    Become a dog that's mad: then is it sin
      To rush into the secret house of death
      Ere death dare come to us? How do you, women?
      What, what! good cheer! Why, how now, Charmian?
      My noble girls! Ah, women, women, look!

59 *woo't* wilt thou  64 *garland . . . war* flower of all soldiers  65 *pole* North
Star (?)  66 *odds* standard of measurement  75 *chares* chores  79–80
*Patience . . . mad* both patience and sorrow are now beside the point

Our lamp is spent, it's out! Good sirs, take heart:          85
We'll bury him; and then, what's brave, what's noble,
Let's do't after the high Roman fashion,
And make death proud to take us. Come, away.
This case of that huge spirit now is cold.
Ah, women, women! Come; we have no friend          90
But resolution, and the briefest end.

> *Exeunt, bearing off Antony's body.*

*Enter Caesar, Agrippa, Dolabella, Maecenas, [Gallus,*          V, i
*Proculeius,] with his Council of War.*

*Caesar.* Go to him, Dolabella, bid him yield:
  Being so frustrate, tell him he mocks
  The pauses that he makes.
*Dolabella.*                    Caesar, I shall.          *[Exit.]*

> *Enter Decretas, with the sword of Antony.*

*Caesar.* Wherefore is that? And what art thou that dar'st
  Appear thus to us?
*Decretas.*                 I am called Decretas.          5
  Mark Antony I served, who best was worthy
  Best to be served. Whilst he stood up and spoke,
  He was my master, and I wore my life
  To spend upon his haters. If thou please
  To take me to thee, as I was to him          10
  I'll be to Caesar; if thou pleasest not,
  I yield thee up my life.
*Caesar.*                 What is't thou say'st?

---

85 *sirs* i.e. Cleopatra's women   V, i, 2 *frustrate* helpless   2–3 *he mocks . . .
makes* i.e. to delay surrendering is ridiculous

*Decretas.* I say, O Caesar, Antony is dead.

*Caesar.* The breaking of so great a thing should make

15    A greater crack. The round world
   Should have shook lions into civil streets
   And citizens to their dens. The death of Antony
   Is not a single doom, in the name lay
   A moiety of the world.

*Decretas.*                He is dead, Caesar,

20    Not by a public minister of justice
   Nor by a hirèd knife; but that self hand
   Which writ his honor in the acts it did
   Hath, with the courage which the heart did lend it,
   Splitted the heart. This is his sword,

25    I robbed his wound of it: behold it stained
   With his most noble blood.

*Caesar.*              Look you sad, friends?
   The gods rebuke me, but it is tidings
   To wash the eyes of kings.

*Agrippa.*             And strange it is
   That nature must compel us to lament
   Our most persisted deeds.

30 *Maecenas.*           His taints and honors
   Waged equal with him.

*Agrippa.*           A rarer spirit never
   Did steer humanity; but you, gods, will give us
   Some faults to make us men. Caesar is touched.

*Maecenas.* When such a spacious mirror 's set before him,
   He needs must see himself.

35 *Caesar.*            O Antony,
   I have followed thee to this. But we do launch
   Diseases in our bodies. I must perforce

---

16 *civil* city   19 *moiety* half   21 *self* same   30 *persisted* i.e. persisted in
31 *Waged equal with* were evenly balanced in   36 *launch* lance

V, i

Have shown to thee such a declining day
Or look on thine: we could not stall together
In the whole world. But yet let me lament          40
With tears as sovereign as the blood of hearts
That thou, my brother, my competitor
In top of all design, my mate in empire,
Friend and companion in the front of war,
The arm of mine own body, and the heart          45
Where mine his thoughts did kindle – that our stars,
Unreconciliable, should divide
Our equalness to this. Hear me, good friends –

*Enter an Egyptian.*

But I will tell you at some meeter season.
The business of this man looks out of him;          50
We'll hear him what he says. Whence are you?
*Egyptian.* A poor Egyptian yet. The Queen my mistress,
Confined in all she has, her monument,
Of thy intents desires instruction,
That she preparèdly may frame herself          55
To th' way she's forced to.
*Caesar.*                          Bid her have good heart:
She soon shall know of us, by some of ours,
How honorable and how kindly we
Determine for her. For Caesar cannot live
To be ungentle.
*Egyptian.*          So the gods preserve thee!          *Exit.* 60
*Caesar.* Come hither, Proculeius. Go and say
We purpose her no shame: give her what comforts
The quality of her passion shall require,

39 *stall* dwell  41 *sovereign* potent  42 *competitor* partner  43 *In . . . design*
in every lofty enterprise  46 *his* its  50 *looks . . . him* shows in his eyes
63 *passion* grief

143

Lest, in her greatness, by some mortal stroke
65  She do defeat us. For her life in Rome
Would be eternal in our triumph. Go,
And with your speediest bring us what she says
And how you find of her.
*Proculeius.*                    Caesar, I shall.                *Exit.*
*Caesar.* Gallus, go you along. *[Exit Gallus.]* Where's Dola-
bella,
To second Proculeius?
70 *All.*                    Dolabella!
*Caesar.* Let him alone, for I remember now
How he's employed. He shall in time be ready.
Go with me to my tent, where you shall see
How hardly I was drawn into this war,
75  How calm and gentle I proceeded still
In all my writings. Go with me, and see
What I can show in this.                *Exeunt.*

V, ii        *Enter Cleopatra, Charmian, Iras, and Mardian.*

*Cleopatra.* My desolation does begin to make
A better life. 'Tis paltry to be Caesar:
Not being Fortune, he's but Fortune's knave,
A minister of her will. And it is great
5   To do that thing that ends all other deeds,
Which shackles accidents and bolts up change;
Which sleeps, and never palates more the dung,
The beggar's nurse and Caesar's.

66 *eternal* eternally memorable   76 *writings* dispatches (to Antony)
V, ii, 2 *A better life* i.e. a truer estimate of values  3 *knave* servant  7 *dung*
i.e. the fruits of earth, which is everybody's nurse

*Enter, [to the gates of the monument,] Proculeius.*

*Proculeius.* Caesar sends greeting to the Queen of Egypt,
  And bids thee study on what fair demands                    10
  Thou mean'st to have him grant thee.
*Cleopatra.*                                     What's thy name?
*Proculeius.* My name is Proculeius.
*Cleopatra.*                              Antony
  Did tell me of you, bade me trust you, but
  I do not greatly care to be deceived,
  That have no use for trusting. If your master                    15
  Would have a queen his beggar, you must tell him
  That majesty, to keep decorum, must
  No less beg than a kingdom: if he please
  To give me conquered Egypt for my son,
  He gives me so much of mine own as I                    20
  Will kneel to him with thanks.
*Proculeius.*                              Be of good cheer:
  Y' are fall'n into a princely hand, fear nothing.
  Make your full reference freely to my lord,
  Who is so full of grace that it flows over
  On all that need. Let me report to him                    25
  Your sweet dependency, and you shall find
  A conqueror that will pray in aid for kindness,
  Where he for grace is kneeled to.
*Cleopatra.*                              Pray you, tell him
  I am his fortune's vassal, and I send him
  The greatness he has got. I hourly learn                    30
  A doctrine of obedience, and would gladly
  Look him i' th' face.

---

14 *to be deceived* whether I am deceived or not    20 *as* that    23 *Make . . .
reference* entrust your case    27 *pray . . . kindness* ask your aid in naming
kindnesses he can do for you    30 *got* i.e. won from me

*Proculeius.*                  This I'll report, dear lady.
Have comfort, for I know your plight is pitied
Of him that caused it.

                 [*Enter Roman Soldiers into the monument.*]

35    You see how easily she may be surprised.
                                 [*They seize Cleopatra.*]
      Guard her till Caesar come.
*Iras.* Royal Queen!
*Charmian.* O Cleopatra! thou art taken, Queen.
*Cleopatra.* Quick, quick, good hands!    [*Draws a dagger.*]
*Proculeius.*                  Hold, worthy lady, hold!
                                       [*Disarms her.*]
40    Do not yourself such wrong, who are in this
      Relieved, but not betrayed.
*Cleopatra.*                  What, of death too,
      That rids our dogs of languish?
*Proculeius.*                          Cleopatra,
      Do not abuse my master's bounty by
      Th' undoing of yourself: let the world see
45    His nobleness well acted, which your death
      Will never let come forth.
*Cleopatra.*                  Where art thou, death?
      Come hither, come: come, come, and take a queen
      Worth many babes and beggars!
*Proculeius.*                          O, temperance, lady!
*Cleopatra.* Sir, I will eat no meat, I'll not drink, sir —
50    If idle talk will once be necessary —
      I'll not sleep neither. This mortal house I'll ruin,
      Do Caesar what he can. Know, sir, that I
      Will not wait pinioned at your master's court

41 *Relieved* rescued   42 *languish* pain   45 *acted* put into effect   50 *If . . .
necessary* even if I must for the present moment resort to words not acts

146

Nor once be chastised with the sober eye
Of dull Octavia. Shall they hoist me up                          55
And show me to the shouting varletry
Of censuring Rome? Rather a ditch in Egypt
Be gentle grave unto me! Rather on Nilus' mud
Lay me stark-nak'd and let the waterflies
Blow me into abhorring! Rather make                             60
My country's high pyramides my gibbet
And hang me up in chains!
*Proculeius.*                       You do extend
These thoughts of horror further than you shall
Find cause in Caesar.

                    *Enter Dolabella.*

*Dolabella.*                  Proculeius,
What thou hast done thy master Caesar knows,                    65
And he hath sent me for thee. For the Queen,
I'll take her to my guard.
*Proculeius.*                  So, Dolabella,
It shall content me best: be gentle to her.
[*To Cleopatra*] To Caesar I will speak what you shall
    please,
If you'll employ me to him.
*Cleopatra.*                  Say, I would die.                 70
                    *Exit Proculeius [with Soldiers].*
*Dolabella.* Most noble Empress, you have heard of me?
*Cleopatra.* I cannot tell.
*Dolabella.*                  Assuredly you know me.
*Cleopatra.* No matter, sir, what I have heard or known.
    You laugh when boys or women tell their dreams;
    Is't not your trick?
*Dolabella.*            I understand not, madam.               75

56 *varletry* mob   60 *Blow me* make me swell

147

*Cleopatra.* I dreamt there was an Emperor Antony.
    O, such another sleep, that I might see
    But such another man.
*Dolabella.*               If it might please ye —
*Cleopatra.* His face was as the heav'ns, and therein stuck
80    A sun and moon, which kept their course and lighted
    The little O, th' earth.
*Dolabella.*             Most sovereign creature —
*Cleopatra.* His legs bestrid the ocean: his reared arm
    Crested the world: his voice was propertied
    As all the tunèd spheres, and that to friends;
85    But when he meant to quail and shake the orb,
    He was as rattling thunder. For his bounty,
    There was no winter in't: an autumn 'twas
    That grew the more by reaping: his delights
    Were dolphin-like, they showed his back above
90    The element they lived in: in his livery
    Walked crowns and crownets: realms and islands were
    As plates dropped from his pocket.
*Dolabella.*                    Cleopatra —
*Cleopatra.* Think you there was or might be such a man
    As this I dreamt of?
*Dolabella.*         Gentle madam, no.
95 *Cleopatra.* You lie, up to the hearing of the gods.
    But if there be nor ever were one such,
    It's past the size of dreaming: nature wants stuff

81 *The . . . earth* (the generally accepted rendering of a folio reading which
may possibly mean something quite different: *The little o' th' earth*)
83–84 *was propertied As* i.e. made music like  85 *quail* cow  *orb* earth
88–90 *his . . . lived in* i.e. he rose above the pleasures that he lived in as the
dolphin rises above the surface of the sea  91 *crowns and crownets* i.e. kings
and princes  92 *plates* coins  97–100 *nature . . . quite* i.e. nature rarely can
compete with man's imagination in creating outstanding forms of excel-
lence, but if she created an Antony, he would be her masterpiece, outdoing
the unreal images of imagination altogether

To vie strange forms with fancy, yet t' imagine
An Antony were nature's piece 'gainst fancy,
Condemning shadows quite.
*Dolabella.*                    Hear me, good madam.          100
Your loss is as yourself, great; and you bear it
As answering to the weight. Would I might never
O'ertake pursued success but I do feel,
By the rebound of yours, a grief that smites
My very heart at root.
*Cleopatra.*               I thank you, sir.          105
Know you what Caesar means to do with me?
*Dolabella.* I am loath to tell you what I would you knew.
*Cleopatra.* Nay, pray you, sir.
*Dolabella.*                    Though he be honorable —
*Cleopatra.* He'll lead me, then, in triumph?
*Dolabella.* Madam, he will. I know't.          110

  *Flourish. Enter Proculeius, Caesar, Gallus, Maecenas,*
    *[Seleucus,] and others of his Train.*

*All.* Make way there! Caesar!
*Caesar.* Which is the Queen of Egypt?
*Dolabella.* It is the Emperor, madam.          *Cleopatra kneels.*
*Caesar.* Arise! You shall not kneel:
I pray you rise, rise, Egypt.
*Cleopatra.*                    Sir, the gods          115
Will have it thus. My master and my lord
I must obey.
*Caesar.*          Take to you no hard thoughts.
The record of what injuries you did us,
Though written in our flesh, we shall remember
As things but done by chance.

102–3 *Would . . . do* i.e. may I never have success if I do not

149

120 *Cleopatra.*                     Sole sir o' th' world,
    I cannot project mine own cause so well
    To make it clear, but do confess I have
    Been laden with like frailties which before
    Have often shamed our sex.
    *Caesar.*                     Cleopatra, know,
125 We will extenuate rather than enforce.
    If you apply yourself to our intents,
    Which towards you are most gentle, you shall find
    A benefit in this change; but if you seek
    To lay on me a cruelty by taking
130 Antony's course, you shall bereave yourself
    Of my good purposes, and put your children
    To that destruction which I'll guard them from
    If thereon you rely. I'll take my leave.
    *Cleopatra.* And may, through all the world: 'tis yours, and
        we,
135 Your scutcheons and your signs of conquest, shall
    Hang in what place you please. Here, my good lord.
                                    *[Offering a scroll.]*
    *Caesar.* You shall advise me in all for Cleopatra.
    *Cleopatra.* This is the brief of money, plate, and jewels
    I am possessed of. 'Tis exactly valued,
140 Not petty things admitted. Where's Seleucus?
    *Seleucus.* Here, madam.
    *Cleopatra.* This is my treasurer; let him speak, my lord,
    Upon his peril, that I have reserved
    To myself nothing. Speak the truth, Seleucus.
145 *Seleucus.* Madam,
    I had rather seel my lips than to my peril
    Speak that which is not.

121 *project* set forth  125 *enforce* emphasize (them)  126 *apply* conform
135 *scutcheons* victor's trappings  138 *brief* résumé  146 *seel* sew up

*Cleopatra.*                    What have I kept back?
*Seleucus.* Enough to purchase what you have made known.
*Caesar.* Nay, blush not, Cleopatra, I approve
  Your wisdom in the deed.
*Cleopatra.*                    See, Caesar: O, behold,          150
  How pomp is followed! Mine will now be yours,
  And should we shift estates, yours would be mine.
  The ingratitude of this Seleucus does
  Even make me wild. O slave, of no more trust
  Than love that's hired! What, goest thou back? Thou
    shalt                                                        155
  Go back, I warrant thee; but I'll catch thine eyes,
  Though they had wings. Slave, soulless villain, dog!
  O rarely base!
*Caesar.*          Good Queen, let us entreat you.
*Cleopatra.* O Caesar, what a wounding shame is this,
  That thou vouchsafing here to visit me,                       160
  Doing the honor of thy lordliness
  To one so meek, that mine own servant should
  Parcel the sum of my disgraces by
  Addition of his envy. Say, good Caesar,
  That I some lady trifles have reserved,                       165
  Immoment toys, things of such dignity
  As we greet modern friends withal; and say
  Some nobler token I have kept apart
  For Livia and Octavia, to induce
  Their mediation — must I be unfolded                          170
  With one that I have bred? The gods! It smites me
  Beneath the fall I have. *[to Seleucus]* Prithee go hence,
  Or I shall show the cinders of my spirits

151 *Mine* i.e. my followers   152 *estates* positions   163 *Parcel* piece out
further   165 *lady* feminine   166 *Immoment* of no moment   167 *modern*
common   171 *With* by   173 *cinders* burning coals

Through th' ashes of my chance. Wert thou a man,
Thou wouldst have mercy on me.

175 *Caesar.*                              Forbear, Seleucus.

                                        [*Exit Seleucus.*]

*Cleopatra.* Be it known that we, the greatest, are misthought
For things that others do; and, when we fall,
We answer others' merits in our name,
Are therefore to be pitied.

*Caesar.*                              Cleopatra,
180 Not what you have reserved, nor what acknowledged,
Put we i' th' roll of conquest: still be't yours,
Bestow it at your pleasure, and believe
Caesar 's no merchant, to make prize with you
Of things that merchants sold. Therefore be cheered,
185 Make not your thoughts your prisons: no, dear Queen,
For we intend so to dispose you as
Yourself shall give us counsel. Feed and sleep:
Our care and pity is so much upon you
That we remain your friend; and so adieu.

*Cleopatra.* My master, and my lord!

190 *Caesar.*                              Not so. Adieu.

                    *Flourish. Exeunt Caesar, and his Train.*

*Cleopatra.* He words me, girls, he words me, that I should
    not
Be noble to myself! But hark thee, Charmian.

                                   [*Whispers Charmian.*]

*Iras.* Finish, good lady, the bright day is done,
And we are for the dark.

---

174 *chance* fortune   176 *misthought* misjudged   178 *merits . . . name* mis-
deeds done in our name (as if Seleucus had falsified the inventory for his
own gain)   182 *Bestow* use   183 *make prize* haggle   185 *Make . . . prisons*
i.e. only in your own conception are you a prisoner   186 *you* of you   191
*words* deceives with words   192 *noble* i.e. by suicide

*Cleopatra.*                    Hie thee again:
  I have spoke already, and it is provided;                    195
  Go put it to the haste.
*Charmian.*              Madam, I will.

*Enter Dolabella.*

*Dolabella.* Where is the Queen?
*Charmian.*                    Behold, sir.          *[Exit.]*
*Cleopatra.*                         Dolabella!
*Dolabella.* Madam, as thereto sworn, by your command
  (Which my love makes religion to obey)
  I tell you this: Caesar through Syria                    200
  Intends his journey, and within three days
  You with your children will he send before.
  Make your best use of this. I have performed
  Your pleasure, and my promise.
*Cleopatra.*                         Dolabella,
  I shall remain your debtor.
*Dolabella.*                I your servant.              205
  Adieu, good Queen; I must attend on Caesar.
*Cleopatra.* Farewell, and thanks.        *Exit [Dolabella].*
                    Now, Iras, what think'st thou?
  Thou, an Egyptian puppet, shall be shown
  In Rome as well as I: mechanic slaves
  With greasy aprons, rules, and hammers shall              210
  Uplift us to the view. In their thick breaths,
  Rank of gross diet, shall we be enclouded,
  And forced to drink their vapor.
*Iras.*                         The gods forbid!
*Cleopatra.* Nay, 'tis most certain, Iras. Saucy lictors
  Will catch at us like strumpets, and scald rhymers       215
  Ballad us out o' tune. The quick comedians

212 *Rank of* offensive because of   214 *lictors* officers   215 *scald* scabby

153

Extemporally will stage us, and present
Our Alexandrian revels: Antony
Shall be brought drunken forth, and I shall see
220 Some squeaking Cleopatra boy my greatness
I' th' posture of a whore.

Iras.                              O the good gods!

Cleopatra. Nay, that's certain.

Iras. I'll never see't! for I am sure my nails
Are stronger than mine eyes.

Cleopatra.                              Why, that's the way
225 To fool their preparation, and to conquer
Their most absurd intents.

*Enter Charmian.*

                              Now, Charmian!
Show me, my women, like a queen: go fetch
My best attires. I am again for Cydnus,
To meet Mark Antony. Sirrah Iras, go.
230 Now, noble Charmian, we'll dispatch indeed,
And when thou hast done this chare, I'll give thee leave
To play till doomsday. – Bring our crown and all.
                              *[Exit Iras.] A noise within.*
Wherefore's this noise?

*Enter a Guardsman.*

Guardsman.                    Here is a rural fellow
That will not be denied your Highness' presence:
235 He brings you figs.

Cleopatra. Let him come in.          *Exit Guardsman.*
                              What poor an instrument
May do a noble deed! He brings me liberty.

220 *squeaking* i.e. because women's parts were acted by young boys  *boy*
satirize  231 *chare* chore

154

My resolution 's placed, and I have nothing
Of woman in me: now from head to foot
I am marble-constant: now the fleeting moon                    240
No planet is of mine.

*Enter Guardsman and Clown [with basket].*

*Guardsman.*             This is the man.
*Cleopatra.* Avoid, and leave him.      *Exit Guardsman.*
   Hast thou the pretty worm of Nilus there,
   That kills and pains not?
*Clown.* Truly I have him; but I would not be the party 245
   that should desire you to touch him, for his biting is
   immortal: those that do die of it do seldom or never
   recover.
*Cleopatra.* Remember'st thou any that have died on't?
*Clown.* Very many, men and women too. I heard of one 250
   of them no longer than yesterday; a very honest woman,
   but something given to lie, as a woman should not do
   but in the way of honesty – how she died of the biting
   of it, what pain she felt. Truly, she makes a very good
   report o' th' worm; but he that will believe all that they 255
   say shall never be saved by half that they do; but this is
   most falliable, the worm 's an odd worm.
*Cleopatra.* Get thee hence, farewell.
*Clown.* I wish you all joy of the worm.
                           *[Sets down his basket.]*
*Cleopatra.* Farewell.                    260
*Clown.* You must think this, look you, that the worm
   will do his kind.

238 *placed* fixed   241 S.D. *Clown* rustic   242 *Avoid* go   243 *worm* serpent
(asp)   247 *immortal* mortal, i.e. deadly (the rustic blunders in speech here
and below)   251 *honest* respectable   257 *falliable* (an error for 'infallible')
262 *his kind* i.e. what may be expected from his species

*Cleopatra.* Ay, ay; farewell.

*Clown.* Look you, the worm is not to be trusted but in the
265  keeping of wise people: for indeed there is no goodness
in the worm.

*Cleopatra.* Take thou no care, it shall be heeded.

*Clown.* Very good. Give it nothing, I pray you, for it is
not worth the feeding.

270  *Cleopatra.* Will it eat me?

*Clown.* You must not think I am so simple but I know the
devil himself will not eat a woman: I know that a
woman is a dish for the gods, if the devil dress her not.
But truly, these same whoreson devils do the gods great
275  harm in their women; for in every ten that they make,
the devils mar five.

*Cleopatra.* Well, get thee gone, farewell.

*Clown.* Yes, forsooth. I wish you joy o' th' worm.    *Exit.*

*[Enter Iras with a robe, crown, etc.]*

*Cleopatra.* Give me my robe, put on my crown, I have
280  Immortal longings in me. Now no more
The juice of Egypt's grape shall moist this lip.
Yare, yare, good Iras; quick. Methinks I hear
Antony call: I see him rouse himself
To praise my noble act. I hear him mock
285  The luck of Caesar, which the gods give men
To excuse their after wrath. Husband, I come:
Now to that name my courage prove my title!
I am fire, and air; my other elements
I give to baser life. So, have you done?

273 *dress* (with pun on the culinary sense)  282 *Yare* nimbly  288 *fire, and*
*air* (the lighter of the four elements, thought of as belonging to immor-
tality)  *other elements* i.e. water and earth, the heavier elements, bequeathed
by Cleopatra to mortality

Come then, and take the last warmth of my lips.          290
Farewell, kind Charmian, Iras, long farewell.
                    *[Kisses them. Iras falls and dies.]*
Have I the aspic in my lips? Dost fall?
If thou and nature can so gently part,
The stroke of death is as a lover's pinch,
Which hurts, and is desired. Dost thou lie still?        295
If thus thou vanishest, thou tell'st the world
It is not worth leave-taking.
*Charmian.* Dissolve, thick cloud, and rain, that I may say
    The gods themselves do weep.
*Cleopatra.*                        This proves me base:
    If she first meet the curlèd Antony,                 300
    He'll make demand of her, and spend that kiss
    Which is my heaven to have. Come, thou mortal wretch,
            *[To an asp, which she applies to her breast.]*
    With thy sharp teeth this knot intrinsicate
    Of life at once untie. Poor venomous fool,
    Be angry, and dispatch. O, couldst thou speak,       305
    That I might hear thee call great Caesar ass
    Unpolicied!
*Charmian.*    O Eastern star!
*Cleopatra.*                    Peace, peace!
    Dost thou not see my baby at my breast,
    That sucks the nurse asleep?
*Charmian.*                    O, break! O, break!
*Cleopatra.* As sweet as balm, as soft as air, as gentle –   310
    O Antony! Nay, I will take thee too:
                    *[Applies another asp to her arm.]*
    What should I stay –                        *Dies.*
*Charmian.* In this wild world? So, fare thee well.

292 *aspic* asp    303 *intrinsicate* intricate    305 *dispatch* make haste    307
*Unpolicied* outwitted

Now boast thee, death, in thy possession lies
315 A lass unparalleled. Downy windows, close;
And golden Phoebus never be beheld
Of eyes again so royal! Your crown 's awry;
I'll mend it, and then play —

*Enter the Guard, rustling in.*

1. *Guardsman.* Where 's the Queen?
*Charmian.*                    Speak softly, wake her not.
1. *[Guardsman].* Caesar hath sent —
320 *Charmian.*                    Too slow a messenger.
                                        *[Applies an asp.]*
O, come apace, dispatch, I partly feel thee.
1. *[Guardsman].* Approach, ho! All 's not well: Caesar 's
    beguiled.
2. *[Guardsman].* There's Dolabella sent from Caesar. Call
    him.
1. *[Guardsman].* What work is here! Charmian, is this
    well done?
325 *Charmian.* It is well done, and fitting for a princess
    Descended of so many royal kings.
    Ah, soldier!                    *Charmian dies.*

*Enter Dolabella.*

*Dolabella.* How goes it here?
2. *Guardsman.*              All dead.
*Dolabella.*                    Caesar, thy thoughts
    Touch their effects in this: thyself art coming
330 To see performed the dreaded act which thou
    So sought'st to hinder.

---

317 s.d. *Enter . . . in* (folio adds 'and Dolabella')   322 *beguiled* tricked
329 *Touch their effects* meet fulfillment

*Enter Caesar and all his Train, marching.*

*All.*                          A way there, a way for Caesar!
*Dolabella.* O sir, you are too sure an augurer:
    That you did fear is done.
*Caesar.*                        Bravest at the last,
    She levelled at our purposes, and being royal,
    Took her own way. The manner of their deaths?      335
    I do not see them bleed.
*Dolabella.*                    Who was last with them?
*1. Guardsman.* A simple countryman, that brought her figs.
    This was his basket.
*Caesar.*              Poisoned, then.
*1. Guardsman.*                    O Caesar,
    This Charmian lived but now, she stood and spake;
    I found her trimming up the diadem                 340
    On her dead mistress; tremblingly she stood,
    And on the sudden dropped.
*Caesar.*                    O noble weakness!
    If they had swallowed poison, 'twould appear
    By external swelling; but she looks like sleep,
    As she would catch another Antony                  345
    In her strong toil of grace.
*Dolabella.*                    Here on her breast
    There is a vent of blood, and something blown;[1]
    The like is on her arm.
*1. Guardsman.* This is an aspic's trail, and these fig leaves
    Have slime upon them, such as th' aspic leaves     350
    Upon the caves of Nile.
*Caesar.*              Most probable
    That so she died: for her physician tells me

334 *levelled at* guessed   346 *toil* net   347 *vent* discharge   *blown* swelled

She hath pursued conclusions infinite
Of easy ways to die. Take up her bed,
355 And bear her women from the monument.
She shall be buried by her Antony.
No grave upon the earth shall clip in it
A pair so famous. High events as these
Strike those that make them; and their story is
360 No less in pity than his glory which
Brought them to be lamented. Our army shall
In solemn show attend this funeral,
And then to Rome. Come, Dolabella, see
High order in this great solemnity.     *Exeunt omnes.*

353 *conclusions* experiments   357 *clip* clasp   359 *Strike* touch